Approaches to Prayer

Approaches to Prayer

A Resource Book
for Groups and Individuals

Edited by
Henry Morgan

Illustrated by
Cathy Stonard

First published in Great Britain 1991
SPCK
Holy Trinity Church
Marylebone Road
London NW1 4DU

Third impression 1995

British Library Cataloguing in Publication Data
Morgan, Henry
Approaches to prayer.
I. Title
242
ISBN 0–281–04557–7

Photoset and printed in Great Britain by
The Longdunn Press Ltd, Bristol.

Contents

The Road goes ever on and on
Down from the door where it began
Now far ahead the Road has gone
And I must follow if I can,
Pursuing it with weary feet
Until it joins some larger way
Where many paths and errands meet
And whither then? The Road goes ever on and on
And whither then? I cannot say.

J. R. R. TOLKIEN

Introduction

Beginnings

If a man does not keep pace with his companions, perhaps it is because he hears a different drummer. Let him step to the music he hears, however measured or far away.

HENRY DAVID THOREAU

SPIDIR is an organization based in South London, whose aim is to further the work of spiritual direction. Its ethos has been discussed in some detail in Gordon Jeff's book, *Spiritual Direction for Every Christian* (SPCK 1987), but in essence SPIDIR's concern is with the idea that many ordinary Christians will value finding another Christian with whom they meet from time to time to reflect together upon their pilgrimage of faith. SPIDIR has sought to promote this idea in a number of different ways. Since the publication of Gordon's book in 1987, he and Dorothy Nicholson, both of whom have been involved with SPIDIR from the beginning, have been sought out by many Christians for advice and help in setting up similar but independent groups in other parts of the country.

Towards the end of 1988 the SPIDIR Committee was discussing ways of celebrating SPIDIR's tenth birthday – the exact date of the first one remains a mystery, but it appears to be somewhere around 1979! The idea emerged that one way of marking this anniversary might be to offer to the Diocese of Southwark – in whose womb, so to speak, SPIDIR was conceived – a Lent Book for 1990, consisting of prayer exercises which people associated with SPIDIR had found helpful. A sort of 'SPIDIR's Greatest Hits'!

We tested the idea out on the Bishop of Southwark, and he encouraged us to pursue it further, so our work began. A small sub-committee was formed. It was agreed that we should each bring to our first meeting a prayer exercise that we had found personally helpful. I naïvely assumed that while these would use different images and ideas, they would nevertheless conform to a fairly standard shape or pattern, i.e. the one that I used! This was not at all the case: they were each very different. Good, but different. My easy assumption that in the book we would offer one, or maybe two, outline prayer sessions, with a number of prayer exercises that could be simply slotted into them, was blown to pieces. Each of the exercises we began with presupposed a different shape for the meeting.

At that point we made a decision which, for better or worse, has crucially influenced the shape of this book. We decided that in inviting contributions

we would lay down no guidelines, save that the prayer exercise needed to be one that the contributor had himself or herself found helpful. We drew up an initial list of people associated with SPIDIR over its brief history, to whom we then wrote asking for a prayer exercise. We tried to make sure that our initial list had a reasonable spread of people – men and women, ordained and lay, black and white, suburban and inner-city, from all shades of churchmanship. Having written, we sat back and waited.

The responses came in quite quickly. People were very generous with their time and energies. But what amazed us was the astonishing diversity of the responses; very few duplicated each other, and the range of ideas and ways into prayer was simply staggering. We decided to edit the responses as little as possible, although some needed editing to make them accessible; we felt that to be truthful to the range of material offered we had to try to pass it on very much as we had received it. The disadvantage of this was going to be a certain unevenness, even perhaps a disjointedness, in the overall presentation. But the advantage of letting so much diverse material stand together seemed to us to outweigh the disadvantage. Authenticity triumphed over neatness. Or so we hope.

Two other things also became clear at about this time. First, that we had been optimistic to aim for Lent 1990: 1992 was more realistic. Secondly that it seemed to us that we potentially had a very interesting book in the making – even perhaps a national publication rather than a Diocesan Lent Book.

The next stage was to order the prayer exercises into chapters. In some cases this was fairly easy, but in others it was less so. Some exercises might have gone into any of several different chapters. Some chapter subjects merge into each other. But we nonetheless hope that the chapter classification will make it easier for readers to find their way around the book. The other useful bonus of this stage was that we identified some

4

obvious gaps: some subjects, some methods that were not so far represented. Where we were able to do so we invited people to fill these gaps for us. Gaps obviously still remain, but we had to call a halt somewhere, and maybe if our book is found to be of value, somebody else will produce a second volume!

The last evolutionary stage in the book's development occurred when we actually showed our text to Philip Law at SPCK. He had a number of helpful and creative suggestions to make. One of them was that we should write the book so that it could readily be used by people on their own. Up to that point we had been thinking of the book as a resource book for leaders of prayer groups, and the exercises had been written up presupposing group usage. But Philip's idea seemed a good one. So we have made the necessary adaptations to most of the prayer exercises so that they can be used by just one person. *Some, however, do need to be done in a group – these are indicated by a circle in the margin.* In practice, with a bit of wit and imagination, it is usually possible to adapt a prayer exercise from individual to corporate use, and vice versa.

Two final points. Firstly, the exercises in this book do vary enormously. Some are very simple and easy. Others, people may find difficult or even threatening. Their authenticity for us lies in the fact that each has been offered by a mature Christian as something they have found of value. But they are not written on tablets of stone. You may want to use some of them just as they are, but you don't have to. You can take bits of an exercise rather than all of it. Reading these exercises may, almost certainly in time will, stimulate you to produce your own. What we are trying to offer here is not the finished product, but an interesting point of departure.

The second point is the most important in the whole book. When you sit or kneel down to pray it is not you who are praying, but the Spirit of God who prays in and through and with you. So don't worry too much about mistakes, or your shortcomings. Do the best you can, and trust the Spirit of God to use it to the glory of God and the building up of God's people. Let me end by telling you a story.

A group of Christians had met together to pray. They talked about what they were to do, and inevitably they disagreed amongst themselves. So they decided, each of them in their own way, to pray for guidance. When they had finished one of the members said that he felt sure that his prayer had been answered: Jesus would be with them when next they met and would show them what to do. Some were sceptical about this but none had the courage to oppose.

Sure enough when they met a week later, suddenly there was Jesus in their midst. 'I expect you all know the prayer I taught my disciples?' he asked. They all nodded. 'And you believe and trust in the Holy Spirit?' he asked. Again they nodded. 'Then there's nothing for me to add,' said Jesus and disappeared.

They were mystified and not greatly edified by this. The bright spark whose idea this had been was asked to pray again. He did so. 'Jesus will join us again next week,' he announced.

A week later Jesus was again in their midst. 'I expect you all know the prayer I taught my disciples?' he asked. They all shook their heads. 'And you believe and trust in the Holy Spirit?' he asked. Again they shook their heads. 'Well you're too ignorant for me to waste my time on,' said Jesus and disappeared.

At this point they became quite irritated, angry even with the bright spark whose idea this was. He was asked to pray for a third time, and when he then announced 'Jesus will join us again next week', they laid their plans.

Sure enough a week later, there was Jesus in their midst. 'I expect you all know the prayer I taught my disciples?' he asked. Forewarned, half the group nodded, whilst half shook their heads. 'Do you believe and trust in the Holy Spirit?' he asked. Again forewarned, half the group nodded and half shook their heads. 'Well,' said Jesus,' those of you who do know and believe had better help those of you who don't.' And he disappeared.

SPIDIR is very much a collective action of a large number of amateurs. Partly to underline that fact, and partly to give credit where credit is due, we would like to thank the following without whose help this book would not have been produced: the Bishop of Southwark – for his encouragement and some small funding, when necessary, for printing and postage; the contributors who are listed separately; the following typists and word processor operators: Anne Bennett, Doreen Cox, Terri Dupe, Caroline Goldsmith, and Lynne Rainey; Cathy Stonard who did the illustrations, and Jean Moore.

Our editorial group began with six: Nigel Godfrey, Viera Gray, Gordon Jeff, Martin Kitchen, Henry Morgan and Dorothy Nicholson. Martin had to drop out about half-way through, due to pressure of other work. Tragically Viera was killed in an accident, early on in our labours, and it is to her that we would like to dedicate this book.

It is not the different practice from one another that breaks the peace and unity, but the judging of one another because of different practices . . . . And here is the true unity in the Spirit, in the inward life, and not in an outward uniformity . . . . And oh, how pleasing it is to the truly spiritual eye to see several sorts of believers, several forms of Christians in the school of Christ, every one learning their own lesson, performing their own particular service, and knowing, owning and loving one another in their several places.

ISAAC PENNINGTON

List of Contributors

Tim Beaumont
Rodney Bomford
John Caldicott
Raymond Chapman
Sandra Conway
M. Davies
Michael Elfred
Hilary Elliott
Sally Eng
Anna Evans
Alan Gadd
Nigel Godfrey
Viera Gray
Alan Harrison
John Hawkins
Ted Hoare
Mary Holliday
Joyce Huggett
Jan Hughes
Jenny Hunt
David Jackson
Gordon Jeanes

Gordon Jeff
Sue King
Martin Kitchen
Anne Long
Leonard Lunn
Richard Maxwell
Henry Morgan
Dorothy Nicholson
Roy Nicholson
Lawrence Osborne
Sandra Pollerman
Nina Putman
Wendy Saunders
Graham Smith
Tessa Spanton
Ann Stricklen
Anne Townsend
Janet Unwin
Darrell Weyman
Frances Wilkinson
Jennifer Zarek

1
Centring Down

When thou disposest thee to think of God, if thy heart be dull and dark, and feels neither wit nor savour nor devotion for to think of God, but only a bare desire and weak will that thou wouldst think of God, then I hope it is good to thee that thou strive not much with thyself as if thou wouldst by thine own might overcome thyself.

WALTER HILTON

Introduction

There are times when prayer comes spontaneously: in a dire emergency, an arrow prayer for help; when something lovely or pleasurable has happened, a warm 'thank you' to God; on realizing meanness or selfishness, a prayer for forgiveness; in the face of beauty or wonder, a prayer of awe and adoration.

One part of growth in prayer is a greater awareness of the activity of God around us and in us so that those brief arrow prayers become an ever-increasing part of our life – an ever more constant being in touch with God.

When we come to a prayer group, however, or when we have set aside a particular time for personal prayer, or for that matter when we go to church, our minds or our emotions may be preoccupied or agitated. In these conditions it would be unrealistic to think that we can start praying immediately. It is hard to see how anyone can arrive in church thirty seconds before a service and expect to give full attention to God.

So it will be wise to begin any special time for prayer with a time for centring down – letting go of worries and distractions and trying to be attentive to the reality of God around us and within us. Some of us will regard this centring down as prayer-in-itself; others may regard it simply as a preparation for prayer. No matter. For all of us it is important.

Some of the suggestions in this chapter have affinities with more extended exercises elsewhere in this book. Essentially what so easily happens is that our bodies, our minds or our emotions somehow get in the way between God and us; whereas when we are properly centred down those same bodies, minds and emotions will all be *helping* us rather than *hindering* our being aware of God and serving him.

Reference is made both in this chapter and elsewhere in the book to relaxing the body. Many will find this helpful. There are, however, others

11

for whom relaxation of the body is not a helpful way into prayer. Again, no matter. Then there are yet others for whom relaxation simply spells *going to sleep*! Let's say at once that there are far, far worse ways of spending prayer time than in going to sleep. Many of us work stupidly long hours and God may actually be trying to tell us to slow down and rest and take life a bit more gently. On the other hand, for some people *awareness* may be more helpful than *relaxation*. Where it is suggested in what follows that we *relax* (and some people simply cannot relax in this way, even after they have tried tensing muscles and then letting go), we try rather to *be aware* of those areas of our body where we are tensed up. For many that simple awareness will help greatly towards relaxation as a kind of by-product, but without sending us to sleep.

Awareness is probably also the key to calming down our emotions and our ever active minds. Try sitting and attempting for a short period to empty yourself of all thoughts and feelings. When, as will inevitably happen very soon, you find a feeling or an idea coming to you, *name* the feeling or thought: *'I am thinking that . . .'* or *'I am feeling . . .'*. By *naming* the thought or the feeling you will begin to have power over it and begin to defuse it.

Nature abhors a vacuum. This is true of prayer. It is virtually impossible – even if it were desirable – totally to empty the mind. Remember the gospel story of the room swept clean of devils into which ten devils worse than the first were able to come. Unless we are quite far along the path of prayer and have a spiritual guide, it is important to take into the silence a word, a phrase from the Bible, or a symbol, a picture. That will keep us safe.

Finally, a word about distractions: these will remain with us till the end of our lives, though the nature of them may alter as we go on. In essence there are two general ways of dealing with distractions. We can gently, without any sense of anger or frustration, turn our minds back to the task in hand. This is rather like the driver of a motor car seeing fascinating things on either side of the road, but realizing that safe driving means ignoring them and turning back to the task in hand. Alternatively, and this is a matter for individual judgement, we could argue that the distractions may sometimes not be distractions at all, but that they are matters of importance to us, that God may wish us to give them our attention and *pray* about them (not simply *fuss* about them) before turning back to our task.

Attentiveness to breathing is a further way of countering distractions – to give total attention to your breathing for a short while when a distraction comes to you before returning to whatever you were trying to do in your prayer. This is especially helpful if you are using only a single word or a short phrase in a contemplative way, for you can simply transfer your attention from the breathing to 'breathing in' the word or phrase so that it becomes assimilated in the very depths of your being. Many Christians would say that simple attentiveness to breathing is a kind of prayer in itself. Breath in the Old Testament is a symbol of the life God gives us: without breathing we should be dead. As we breathe, we breathe in the very life of God himself.

Here then are some suggestions which have been offered to us for 'ways into prayer' and three prayer exercises which use awareness as the focus for prayer.

Leads into silence

There are many ways of leading into silence with the intention of focusing ourselves to wait upon God. They are often words received by the mind, but it can be useful to try to focus the senses, the body. One of the most immediate distractions to the recollected mind is the body's clamour for attention; and one of the simplest ways to still the mind is to concentrate it on the senses.

(1) Feeling or touch

Simple physical actions such as the following:

Stand or sit on the floor with legs stretched out in front – try to touch the toes. It doesn't matter how near (or not) one gets. Reach as far as possible, then *stop*, breathe out, and relax into that stretch. After a few seconds reach again, a little further, then stop and relax. Always be gentle.

The 'tree' posture: stand upright and raise one leg so that the foot rests against the other knee (with the raised knee out to one side); then slowly raise the hands above the head and circle to the sides and down, breathing deeply.

The exact actions don't matter. If the body learns to stay where it is put, even balanced on one leg, it will more easily sit still when composed for prayer. A posture which is only used for prayer – such as kneeling,

13

or sitting cross-legged on the floor –
can come to prompt 'do not disturb'
messages automatically.

(2) Smell – the breath

Burning incense or 'room fragrance'
oils prompt awareness of the breath;
breathe in deeply and out very gently
'as if a feather is under your nose
and you don't want to disturb it'.
Think of breathing in the Spirit and
breathing out sin and hurt. The
rhythm of breathing can be matched
to a rhythmic prayer: perhaps the
whole 'Jesus Prayer' (Lord Jesus
Christ, Son of God, have mercy
upon me a sinner) or just 'Jesus' (in)
'mercy' (out).

(3) Hearing

The sound of a small bell, or something similar, is a clear sound which
rings on and gradually dies away.
Focus on it, really listen to the sound
and follow it into silence as it dies
away. It is still ringing, but too
quietly to be heard. The sound can
be repeated at intervals if it is
helpful to recall the wandering mind.

(4) Sight

Visual focuses are many and various:
a lighted candle, an icon, a few
flowers, a few pebbles in a bowl of
water. According to temperament,
they offer associated ideas for meditation, or a mental image when the
eyes are closed.

As so often, it has all been said much better elsewhere. This poem has been a valued 'lead in' to prayer, and points in turn to the physical 'fingering', to breath, to listening. It works well if 'Say the prayer again' is substituted for 'Play the tune again'.

A Lesson in Music

Play the tune again: but this time
with more regard for the movement at the source of it
and less attention to time. Time
 falls
curiously in the course of it.

Play the tune again: not watching
your fingering, but forgetting,
 letting flow
the sound till it surrounds you.
 Do not count
or even think. Let go.

Play the tune again: but try to be
nobody, nothing, as though the
 pace
of the sound were your heart
 beating, as though
the music were your face.

Play the tune again: It should be
 easier
to think less every time of the
 notes, of the measure.
It is all an arrangement of silence.
 Be silent, and then
play it for your pleasure.

Play the tune again: and this time
 when it ends,
do not ask me what I think. Feel
 what is happening
strangely in the room as the sound
 glooms over
you, me, everything.

Now,
play the tune again.

– from 'Weathering' by Alastair Read,
(Canongate Publishing, 16 Frederick Street,
Edinburgh EH2 2HB, 1978)

○ (5) A prayer exercise to help people begin an evening meeting

The purpose of this exercise is to help people shed the load they have carried through the day by offering it to God, and having done that, to become present to God, to each other, and to themselves.

– Begin by becoming relaxed, letting go of all tension in the body, beginning with the toes and working up through the body to the face. Most tension is felt in the shoulders, so pay special attention to this area. The spine should stretch gently up, not ramrod straight, but alert. Relax the area round the mouth and the frown line between the eyes. On the outward breath, let go of any remaining tension, and on the inward breath, ask the Holy Spirit to renew you.

– In imagination, return to your front door, and review the events of

15

the day. Thank God for all the good things that have come your way today. Forgive anyone who has injured or hurt you. Hand over to God any anxieties or problems you are carrying. Ask forgiveness where necessary, and thank God for his love.

– Still in imagination, go to a peaceful place in the country, perhaps somewhere you know. Feel the warmth of the sun on you, see the green of the grass and trees, the blue of the sky. Find a place by the side of a river or lake and sit down on the grass, or a nearby tree-stump. Let the peace of the place enfold you, and know that God's love is surrounding and filling you. Listen to his word to you:

Those who wait for the Lord shall renew their strength.

– After a few minutes return to the room, become aware of it, and of the people who may be there with you.

(The leader taking the exercise can determine how much time to give to each section.)

---

(6) An awareness walk

The prayer exercise which follows appears at first sight to apply to the countryside, but there is no reason why it should not be used in an urban setting. C. S. Lewis once observed that 'next to the Blessed Sacrament itself, your neighbour is the most holy thing which will ever present itself to the senses'; and in the city there will be many signs, if we are sufficiently aware, of men and women having been open to the Spirit of God. There is also, even in the city, considerable evidence of the natural world burgeoning amidst the concrete, for those who have eyes to see.

Find SPACE alone outside.

Stand STILL and be SILENT. . . .

BREATHE IN the whole scene with eyes, ears, nose and feet.

Be aware of yourself in this scene.

FEEL your limbs, hands, fingers, feet.

LISTEN TO every sound near, mid-distance and far away, in earth and sky.

On your walk record the number of different sounds.

TOUCH as many things on your walk as you can. Use fingers and finger-tips.

FEEL the ground beneath your feet – is it easy walking or difficult?

FEEL the weight of objects. Feel the natural and the man-made.

COLLECT examples of different textures (bark, leaves, stone, wood, paper, metal, plastic, etc.).

TASTE and perhaps chew a blade of grass.

SMELL the countryside, water, earth, animals, food, sun on bricks, shrubs, flowers, cooking, traffic, tar, etc.).

Try and find something with a particular scent and bring it back with you.

LOOK with eyes and the inward eye, seeing with mind, hand and eye.

LOOK DOWN into the earth and the ditches; things near and far. Notice all the different greens; be aware of all the colours.

LOOK UP AT SHAPES against the sky: shadow patterns; shapes of trees, buildings, roof materials, chimneys, road shapes, gardens, people – order and chaos, beauty and ugliness, light and shade, contrasts.

TRY AND FIND A PICTURE from your walk to hold in your memory for recording by prose, poetry, story-telling, painting, drawing, making, creating . . .

CONCENTRATE on some small object – trying to see it as if for the first time.

A reading from Mother Julian

He showed me a little thing, the size of a hazelnut, in the palm of my hand, and it was as round as a ball. I looked at it with my mind's eye and I thought, 'What can this be?' And answer came, 'It is all that is made.' I marvelled that it could last, for I thought it might have crumbled to nothing, it was so small.

And the answer came into my mind, 'It lasts and ever shall because God loves it.' And all things have being through love of God.

In this little thing I saw three truths.

The first is that God made it.

The second is that God loves it.

The third is that God looks after it.

What is he indeed that is maker and lover and keeper? I cannot find words to tell.

(from *Revelations of Divine Love*; this translation from *Enfolded in Love: Daily Readings with Julian of Norwich*, ed. Robert Llewelyn, Darton, Longman and Todd 1980).

(7) Can these bones live?

Centuries ago, the Chinese knew that to have a healthy body one had to have a healthy marrow. By visualizing the breath going through the centre of hollow bones they aimed to encourage the body's natural healing powers. For the Christian 'bone-breathing' is a simple, effective way of bringing in the body as one's best ally in prayer.

Ideally one lies on the floor, flat on the back, relaxing into the floor as much as one can, with arms loosely resting down the sides. It is, however, quite possible to do the exercise in a sitting, or even standing, position, the feet being placed a hip-width apart and firmly 'rooted' on the floor.

(a) Visualize openings in the ends of the toes on the right foot. Breathe out, then on the in-breath visualize the breath coming in through the toes, through the bones of the foot, and draw the breath up through the centre of the bones to the hip.

On the out-breath, breathe out down the centre of the bones and out through the toes. All this should be done slowly.

Do this three times, and then go to the left leg and repeat up and down the left leg three times.

On the fourth breath, breathe up the left leg to the centre of the pelvis and out through the right leg. Do this three times; this forms a bridge between the legs and one is aware of the pelvis connected to the spine, and the legs connected to the pelvis.

Pause for a few moments, breathing normally.

(b) Do the same routine with the arms.

The ends of the fingers open, breathe out and then on the in-breath breathe into the fingers on the right hand and up to the shoulder and out down the arm and out of the fingers. Repeat as before, then go to the left arm. Finally breathe in up the left arm to the centre of the collar bone and breathe out through the right arm, in through the right and out through the left, repeating all this three times.

Pause to breathe normally.

(c) Starting at the base of the spine, breathe in through and up the spine, coming out at the crown of the head and over the head to between the eyebrows. Breathe out down the face, go into the mouth, over the top of the spine and down to the base.

Repeat three times.

Pause to breathe normally.

(d) From the spine, breathe in around each side of the rib cage to the breastbone, and out from the breastbone around each side of the ribs back to the spine, repeating all as before.

18

2
Prayer in the Midst of Life

Earth's crammed with heaven and every common bush afire with God.
But only he who sees takes off his shoes
The rest sit round it and pick blackberries.

ELIZABETH BARRETT BROWNING

Introduction

The Report of the Archbishop of Canterbury's Commission on Urban Priority Areas, *Faith in the City* (Church House Publishing 1985) has some important things to say about worship – many of which are as applicable to non-Urban Priority Areas as they are to UPAs. Thus, worship 'will reflect the concern of local UPA people for things to be more concrete and tangible rather than abstract and theoretical' (ch. 6:104); and again, 'Worship will put the harsh realities in a new light. It may enable people to withdraw for a time from the pressures, but it will be "withdrawal with intent to return", not evasion' (ch. 6:108), and finally, 'Running through all the aspects of UPA life as they need to affect worship is the firm and hopeful recognition of the importance of the ordinary' (ch. 6:109).

This 'importance of the ordinary' is of course a very biblical insight, beginning in the Old Testament with such people as Amos. God spoke to him through the actions of a swarm of locusts (Amos 7.1–3), a man on a building site (7.7–9), and a basket of summer fruit (8.1–3). In the New Testament Jesus constantly sees the truths of God revealed in ordinary things, like the action of a sower, a fisherman, or a shepherd.

The exercises in this chapter all seek to affirm this 'importance of the ordinary' – either by offering something which you can take out into your life and use (as in exercises 1 and 2); or by offering an opportunity to sharpen your awareness of how God speaks through ordinary, everyday events (as in exercises 3–7).

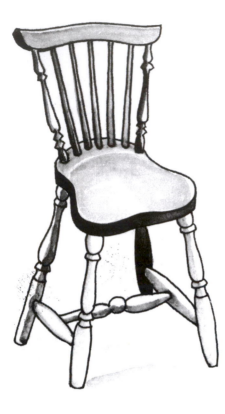

(1) Taking Jesus with you

Sit down, but with an empty chair next to you. Use one of the 'centring down' exercises from earlier in the book.

Then imagine that Jesus has come into the room to join you. What does he look like? Is he tall or short? How old is he? What is he wearing? Imagine the expression on his face. He comes and sits down on the empty chair next to you. He asks you how you are. What do you reply? What do you tell him? What does he reply? When there is a lull in the conversation, he tells you that he has come especially to be with you, and that he intends to stay with you for the rest of your life, although you will not be able to see him. 'Please talk to me whenever you'd like to,' he says, 'for even when you've left this room I will be with you.'

(2) Taking a word or an image with you

A variation on the previous exercise is to use an image, or a story, or a phrase, which you take with you through your life recalling it as often as you can, until your next time of prayer. It could be an icon, or another visual image. It could be a Bible passage, story, or a reading which was used in church the previous Sunday. It could be simply a phrase – a line from the Bible, or from a prayer.

---

(3) Symbolic gestures

The aim of this exercise is to help you identify symbolic gestures, actions, or pithy sayings that you have seen or heard – perhaps, indeed probably, in a very secular context – and then reflect on what they might tell you about God. By extension, the hope is that your awareness of God speaking in this way will be heightened, and you will be more open to receive in the future.

It will probably be helpful to start with an example. You might go to the Bible and do a simple and brief study on the story of Jesus washing his disciples' feet (John 13) – an ordinary, everyday courtesy, which nevertheless carried a powerful truth. Then reflect on why it was necessary for people to have their feet washed. Are there other examples of this custom in the Bible? Who would normally do the washing of others' feet? What precisely would be physically involved? What point was Jesus seeking to make by doing this? How do you think the disciples felt?

Then see if you can identify other ordinary everyday actions from your own experience, which might speak of God.

○ (4) Enacted prayer

Unbeknown to your group, you will have planned to put them into two categories. This could be done quite simply; for example, by asking people to help themselves to a Bible when they come in, some of which have green markers, some of which have yellow markers. People should not be put into categories on any obvious external value such as age, sex or race.

Offer one category of people a really lavish cream cake or something you know to be popular in the group. Ask your chosen category of people to take one, even if they don't want it. The second category will be offered a cream cracker or some other dry biscuit. Then put on a piece of music which symbolizes wealth in contrast to poverty, exploitation or similar. Ask people to eat what they have been given (or leave it on their plate if they don't want it) and to let their thoughts and prayers range freely. You might introduce the meditation with a few simple words such as: 'Seek God's justice.'

Discussion: You might want to unpack people's insights, gently.

People might have exhibited anger, resentment, why me, I can't eat this while others have to go without. I can't not eat, because it looks ungrateful, etc., etc.

Explain to people how they were categorized and share with them something of the pain different groups feel at being excluded in one way or another.

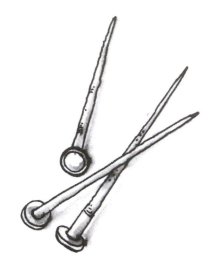

Invite the group to take this experience with them, and to look out for examples of painful categorization in church, at home, at work, or in the community. When you meet next, invite the group to share any examples they have noticed or experienced.

---

(5) The 'slot' prayer

Spend a few minutes with one of the 'centring down' exercises. Then read through the following, slowly, with pauses of a few minutes where indicated.

Imagine that you are at work, at school or college, or about the home – or wherever you spend your working day.

Think of yourself at your desk, sink, or whatever!

PAUSE

Then in your imagination:

STOP what you are doing for just a moment
   – a brief break will relax your mind.

PAUSE

LOOK at the things to hand and the people around you
   – the things are created by God
   – and the people are created in God's image.

PAUSE

OFFER them all, along with yourself as you are, to God
   – God accepts all that we are
   – and all that we offer.

PAUSE

THEN continue, as a prayer, what you have to do
   – work can also be part of prayer
   – it all depends upon what we are prepared to offer.

(6) The last twenty-four hours

After a time of 'centring down', lead into the following exercise:

Spend some time slowly going back over the events of the past twenty-four hours. Recall as much detail as you can: where you were; what you did; what you said; what was said to you; what you said; how you felt, etc.

Reflect on the day as a whole and spend some time on each of the following exercises:

(a) Call to mind two or three things from the day for which you would like to thank God.

(b) Call to mind two or three things from the day which caused you concern, anxiety or worry, and offer them to God.

(c) Call to mind two or three things from the day where you marred God's image in you.

(d) See if you can identify one point during the day where God touched your life: where God was revealed to you; where God spoke to you.

(7) Storytelling

First, read through the exercise, becoming familiar with its shape and objectives. Then choose a comfortable place and body position. Still the body and mind, coming to a quiet inner place. Read or listen to Isaiah 49.8–10, ending with '. . . and one who loves them shall lead them and take them to water at bubbling springs' (NEB).

In our own life story there have been times when we were comforted and led and held close by someone from whom we received much love. Recall one such experience and let it rise up in your memory. Take a few moments and recall the whole story. Pause. Now allow the interior spotlight to focus on one element of the story at a time – ourselves, the situation, the one who came, the feeling of being cherished – focusing on each long enough to extract the full measure of the gift.

At the end of the reflection period, choose one word as a symbol of the story. Use the word to recall the good feelings from the experience and to remember the story.

(8) Transfiguring pain

The aim of this exercise is to encourage you to identify a painful or difficult experience you have had, and then to see how with prayer and faith that experience might be transfigured. You might begin the exercise by

reading this true story, or you might have one of your own – perhaps pausing after each paragraph, and then thinking about it and wondering what truths you might learn from it.

I was once a member of an inner-city church which worshipped on a Sunday in a large room, which was used from Monday to Friday as a classroom in the local comprehensive school. It fell to me to go to the school late on a Friday afternoon to prepare the room for the Sunday worship. Inevitably the floor was dirty and marked and I had to clean it. Often the church furnishings were damaged or left in a mess and I had to rearrange them tidily. I grew to hate Friday afternoons – I used to resent all the mess and dirt I had to clear up – we never left the room messy and dirty for the school when they returned on Monday, so why should they leave it like this for us? The minor acts of vandalism in the room (and in retrospect I can see that they were only minor, but they didn't seem like that at the time!) seemed like a calculated insult to the God we worshipped there on a Sunday. I came to my cleaning task tired after a busy day and usually had the prospect of an evening meeting afterwards. I grew to hate Friday afternoons.

I decided to create some space around my cleaning task. I would plan to have the early part of Friday afternoons off, and I would keep Friday evenings clear, so that I could go home and relax. Over quite a short period of time the cleaning task felt less pressured. All the problems remained the same – but they ceased to be a burden. Gradually I came to find that I looked forward to preparing the room so that it was fit for the worship of God. Others might arrange the flowers, or read the lessons, or make the tea after the service, or count the collection, but my task was to make the room beautiful for God. I grew to look forward to Friday afternoons.

As I reflected on this, I wondered what the difference was between what I was doing on a Friday afternoon after school, and what the school cleaners were doing in the rest of the building. Not much, in fact probably nothing at all. They were making the school 'beautiful for God' just as much as I was. And if that was true of them, it was equally true of the dustmen, and the street sweepers, and the myriads of other men and women with cleaning tasks, on whom society looks down. I found that I had learned to value a vast number of ordinary people who were caring for God's creation, in a way I had not recognized before.

○ (9) Thank you

Thanking is one of the most important parts of prayer; without it prayer can sometimes grow dull and heavy. This is particularly likely in intercessory prayer groups where a long list of people dying from cancer, or people with broken homes, people without jobs, the homeless and the hungry can suck the person praying down into a kind of depression.

But there are always two sides to anything in life, so intercession in a prayer group needs to be balanced with thanksgiving. In prayer groups this may well be verbalized, but the essence of thanking is not *words* but *an attitude to life*. Many years ago *Punch* featured a cartoon of a great long chain gang of slaves engaged in building an Egyptian temple, passing bricks along the line one at a time, and one slave is saying crossly to his next-door neighbour, 'For goodness sake, *stop* saying "thank you" every time.'

Maybe even God might get fed up with repeated routine and the not really felt 'thank you's, but he surely rejoices at *a thankful attitude to life*.

Outline for a group meeting

– Give paper and pens to everyone in the group and invite them to list all the things for which they would like to say 'thank you' to God. Allow a good fifteen minutes of silence for this so that people get past the things uppermost in their minds and go to matters deeper down and further back. Urge people to WRITE, because for most of us to write helps to unblock both the mind and the imagination.

– Have available a very large sheet of paper or card and several tubes of glue. On a table in the centre have some small squares of paper (something like three inches square) along with plenty of coloured felt-tip pens.

– Invite members of the group to take three, four or five small bits of paper each (according to the size of the group and the time available) and draw (or write if they must!) on each piece of paper something to illustrate one area of thankfulness in their life, selected from the longer list they have made.

– When all the drawings are complete, invite the group members to paste their papers to the chart and display it. If some kind of a pattern can be made, so much the better.

– Some of the words and drawings may not make sense, but leave the group to ponder the chart in silence for five minutes or so and then go round the group asking people to explain their own contributions.

– The whole group now prays both with the chart and with the rest of their own list in silence for about ten minutes.

– Finally, the leader names each member of the group in turn, with a minute or two in between each name

27

so that silent thanks can be given for each person, their gifts affirmed and one special extra gift requested for each one. The length of time between each depends, again, on the size of the group and the amount of time available. The leader would do well in this particular prayer session to plan the timing carefully, though allowing some freedom for the Holy Spirit! End with a short spoken prayer, or the Grace said all together, holding hands.

God is not a good habit
  a useful Sunday exercise
  one interest among others
  a fascinating hobby
God is life itself
  He is Someone
  not to be analysed
  examined, proved
  but to be met
And when that happens
  Life unfolds
  meanings matter
  love is deeper
Be still. Relax. Unwind.
Open those inner doors.

HOWARD BOOTH

3
Praying with the Bible

I have sometimes seen more in a line of the Bible than I could well tell how to stand under; and yet at another time the whole Bible hath been to me as dry as a stick.

JOHN BUNYAN

Introduction

Perhaps the most obvious resource for the Christian as he or she comes to pray, is the Bible. It would be possible, no doubt, to produce a book solely given over to different ways of using the Bible like this, and still cover no more than a small number of the possibilities. We can do even less here. What we offer, just as a taste of the range of possibilities, is one fairly traditional method, two scripted meditations on particular biblical passages, a scripted meditation which uses a biblical passage alongside non-biblical material, one very imaginative use of biblical passages, and two exercises which use biblical passages as a starting point from which to begin.

Clearly in this process the dividing line between Bible study on the one hand, and prayer on the other, becomes so indistinct as to be almost indistinguishable.

The exercises may well be best used after some 'centring down' exercises.

(1) Praying the Scriptures

This is a method of prayer going back to the fourth and fifth centuries. Using Scripture as its base, it moves from reading to reflection, prayer and stillness in the presence of God.

reading   Choose a short Scripture passage, read it slowly several times, marking its context; then seek within it the present word of God and his truth.

31

reflection Spend some time (about 10 minutes) taking this word of God, reflecting fully on it, receiving it into your life, and applying it to your own situation and needs.

prayer Then responding to the truth that God has revealed to you through his word, enter into a dialogue with him, in which you listen to him and respond to him, the living presence within the word.

stillness 'Be still and know that I am God'; a period of quiet, to welcome both God's word and God himself afresh into the depths of our lives, reaffirming our unity with him and his will for us. Beginning with a few minutes this period can be extended as you relax into the stillness and are affirmed by it.

The following is an example:

reading Matthew 9.9–13

reflection Jesus came for sinners, so that none of us need ever be discouraged or imagine that we are unworthy of being in the presence of God and of Christ. Ponder afresh on God's gracious assurance of mercy and forgiveness and on Jesus' call to follow him in this same pathway, extending mercy and forgiveness to those who have offended us and following him in the way of the cross.

prayer Respond to this call of Jesus; talk to him, expressing whatever is appropriate in terms of praise and penitence, gratitude and resolve; receiving and offering forgiveness in response to his truth.

stillness Be still and be open to God, open to his peace, joy and love and open to any insights, longings and resolutions that come to your attention, remembering that God himself is love.

The next two meditations should be read aloud slowly:

(2) The peace

Read John 14.27.

Hear Jesus saying: My peace I give to you – not as the world gives, do I give . . . My peace – not the world's peace . . .'

Peace in the World usually signifies a period without conflict – liable to be shattered at any moment – transient, negative, precarious, decaying . . .

God's peace is lasting, positive. Jesus says: 'I am the Prince of Peace . . . I, I myself am peace. I *made* peace through the blood of the cross. It is there I can bring the fragments of life together.'

'It is there I can bring the fragments of *your* life together, making you whole, at one, at peace with yourself and others.'

PAUSE

'And I am *alive*. I journeyed through death. So I am your living peace here and now, every day, whatever happens, so don't let your hearts be troubled or afraid.'

PAUSE

Read John 20.19–23.

After the resurrection Jesus came and stood among the disciples and said: 'Peace be with you. As the Father sent me even so send I you.'

He is here among us. What is he saying to you? Are you willing to be sent as his messenger of peace – near, far, anywhere?

PAUSE

They were filled with joy at seeing the Lord. Then he breathed on them and said: 'Receive the Holy Spirit.'

We find it hard to receive. Let's help each other. When you are ready, open your eyes and look at each other. Say to the person sitting next to you, by name: 'X, Jesus says to *you*, "My peace I give to you." Receive the Holy Spirit.'

PAUSE

Then, praise and worship him in any way appropriate and natural.

Other peace Scriptures

John 20.19–23; Rom. 5.1; Col. 1.20; Phil. 11.6–7; Jer. 6.14, 8.15; Matt. 10.34.

(3) Martha and Mary

Read Luke 10.38–41.

Martha and Mary highlight two aspects of our relationship with Jesus: times to sit quietly with him; times to be active, serving him by loving and serving others.

Imagine the scene. Go into the house. Enter the room where Jesus and Mary are sitting. Join them quietly. Listen. Enjoy being there.

PAUSE

What is the quality of your listening? Has listening to God together in a group helped you? What difference has it made in your own life/ministry of caring?

Relaxation and listening prayers

Return to the room in Bethany. Rest and relax. Listen again. Now see Martha rushing in – loving, eager, practical in her desire to serve Jesus. How do you cope with such interruptions? Could they possibly become means of service and intercession? How?

PAUSE

Jesus was probably tired and wanted some peace and quiet rather than fuss and hassle and special food. Mary was sensitive to this need and tried to meet it. Martha made her own assessment of his needs and priorities.

What has this to teach us in all our contacts with others in need? What is our motive in caring? And its result? Be specific. Ask Jesus to direct us.

PAUSE

We need to be both Martha and Mary and find it difficult to get the balance right. Ask for discernment to know when it is Martha-time and Mary-time. Reflect on your last week's schedule. Ask Jesus for his assessment of it.

PAUSE

Consider the clash of temperaments seen in Martha and Mary. Jot down on paper any current problems, situations or relationships you are finding difficult. Share what you have written with Jesus. Ask for greater insight and wisdom. Be willing to forgive and seek forgiveness.

PAUSE

Is there any action you should take now? Or later? Specifically hand it over to God. If you wish, visualize this by tearing up paper and putting it into the waste-paper basket. Then move into intercession, bringing others, social and world issues, etc. to Jesus as in the home in Bethany.

(4) 'Unless a grain of wheat falls into the earth and dies . . .'

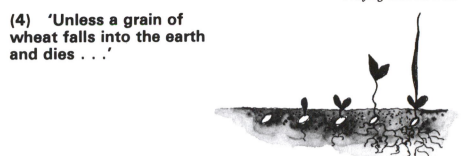

Read out loud John 12.24 –

Truly, truly, I say to you, unless a grain of wheat falls into the earth and dies, it remains alone; but if it dies, it bears much fruit.

Keep a time of silence (10 minutes) to reflect on these words.

Read out loud the poem below. Keep a time of silence, and imagine pictures in your mind, for the words in the poem.

>My Lord will blaze a trail for me
>For he knows and understands
>my needs.
>He will take me to where the
>grass grows green,
>And in the still sparkling water
>He will wash my wounds
>And my soul shall sing.
>
>He will lead me onward,
>sustaining
>Me when my courage fails,
>Holding me safe when my
>footsteps falter
>And my heart shall sing.
>
>Even when the storm clouds
>gather round me
>And the dark wind blows,
>When I can no longer see
>my way
>He shall hold the light steady
>before me
>And protect me from all harm
>With the strength of his hand.

> How blessed am I that the Lord calls
> me his own.
> I shall live out the number of
> my days
> In the light of his presence
>
> And I shall sing. . . .
> JAN HUGHES

Either draw your pictures on a piece of paper *or* mime/dance, one of your pictures.

○ (5)   Resurrection

This takes some preparation. You need to choose a background theme, such as healing, and then to locate some healing stories in the Gospels, for example:

> The woman with the issue of blood (Mark. 5.21–43)
> The thief on the cross (Luke 23.39–43)
> Mary Magdalene (Luke 7.36–50)

Write on a number of pieces of card the reference to the event and the person in that event people are to identify with; clearly you can have two people from the same incident, i.e. you can have the man lowered from the roof and someone from the room (cf. Mark 2:1–12). You can have people with names given and people whose names are unknown to us.

Then in your group:

Give out Bibles if people have not brought their own with them.

Give out the cards randomly.

All these people gathered in this room have met after the death and resurrection of Jesus and are remembering the incident identified in the biblical reference. After a period of quiet when people can reflect on the incident they can share their experience of Jesus.

Later the conversation can continue as appropriate.

Then as people break from that post-resurrection experience let them talk about the experience they have been through.

36

(6) The transfiguration

Reading (15 minutes)

Read Mark 9.2–13 and the following comments, then read the passage again and spend some time meditating upon it. Note down anything which strikes you about this incident.

Jesus is revealed in all his glory: the sharpest possible contrast to the suffering Messiah of just a few weeks later. A contrast but not a contradiction, for the glory which is here revealed is the glory of the resurrection: a glory which can be attained to only by taking the path of suffering and crucifixion.

Nor is this the only way in which the gospel accounts of the Transfiguration allude to Jesus' passion. The disciples who accompany him are the same three who wait with him in Gethsemane. And the subject of his talk with the prophets is his forthcoming crucifixion. Death and transfiguration go hand in hand. The notion of death and transfiguration, or death and resurrection, speaks very powerfully to us at least partly because of our experience of cycles of death and rebirth in different aspects of our daily lives. We will use this idea as the jumping-off point to explore some of the personal changes we are now experiencing.

Making your lists (10 minutes)

(a) Begin by making a list. Aim for at least five items. List the things that you feel are dying in your life, the things you feel diminishing, becoming less important, receding, separating, the things you are losing interest in, letting go of, things that seem just about over. Perhaps you once enjoyed gardening but are beginning to find it drudgery. Perhaps a friendship or a job seems to be coming to an end. Perhaps an old attitude or feeling is changing. Concentrate on things that seem to be passing but are not completely past.

(b) Begin a second list, this time of things that are coming into being, things that are not fully a part of your life but which are rising, emerging, returning, becoming more important, more desirable. This might include a new friendship or job.

Telling your stories (30 minutes)

Take a couple of minutes to look over your completed lists. Select from each list the one item which seems most significant or interesting to you. Tell the story of that which is waxing or waning, your feelings about it, anxieties, anticipations, expectations. Try to let your perceptions and feelings flow freely until they come to a natural conclusion. What is helping or hindering the passing of the old and the emergence of the new? What does this suggest to you?

If you have time, you might like to repeat the process for other items on the list. Do you see any connections between the two lists? If so, you might like to write about this relationship.

Review

Look over what you have written. Make any further notes or comments which suggest themselves. Ask God to show you his active presence in these changes. Does he appear to be pruning away some of these parts of your life in order to make room for fresh growth? (5 minutes)

If this is being done as a group exercise, allow a few minutes for people to share extracts from what they have written *if they wish to do so*. (A journal is essentially private; people should never feel obliged to share what they have written.) It may or may not be appropriate to allow comment on what is shared in this way.

Your insights (or the things shared at this point) can become the basis for a short act of worship, perhaps concluding with the following collect (or similar prayer):

Collect for Easter Eve

Grant, Lord,
that we who are baptized into the death of your Son our Saviour Jesus Christ
may continually put to death our evil desires and be buried with him;
that through the grave and gate of death we may pass to our joyful resurrection;
through his merits, who died and was buried and rose again for us,
your Son Jesus Christ our Lord.

(from the Alternative Service Book 1980)

---

(7) The genealogy of Jesus

(a) Read through the genealogy of Jesus at the beginning of Matthew's Gospel (Matt. 1.1–17).

How many of the names mentioned mean anything? What do you know about any of these people?

You will see that four women are mentioned amongst all the men: who are these women? If you want to look them up, see, for Tamar, Gen. 38.1–3; Rahab, Josh. 2.1–21; Ruth, the Book of Ruth; the wife of Uriah, 2 Sam. 11.

You might also notice Matthew's dilemma when he comes at last to Jesus, who is not described as the others have been, as the son of Joseph. Why not?

If Jesus was not the son of Joseph what is the point of the genealogy anyway?

(b) What the genealogy offers is a sort of spiritual family tree for Jesus. What would a spiritual family tree of our own look like?

Make a list of those who have influenced your inner development either in person, or at second hand, for example through their writings. Remember to include the 'black sheep' – the negative influences – as well. It is possible, if there is time, to work out quite complicated 'relationships', or to consider the shape into which the tree has grown.

The Bible is like a telescope. If a man looks through his telescope, then he sees worlds beyond; but if he looks at his telescope, then he does not see anything but that. The Bible is a thing to be looked through, to see that which is beyond; but most people only look at it; and so they see only the dead letter.

PHILIP BROOKS

4
Imagination and Prayer

Can I imagine Christ praying the prayers I thought of saying tonight or tomorrow?

ANON

Introduction

Several chapters in this book deal indirectly with the more imaginative parts of ourselves. Technology, which surrounds us on every side, has a tendency to make us *literal-minded*, down-to-earth, even unimaginative. And of course we *need* to be practical – efficient administration is just as valuable a gift from God as any other. Christian feet are meant to be kept on the ground just as firmly as any other kind of feet.

But this down-to-earth part of us should not be developed at the expense of our intuitive and imaginative side, our playful side, which does not insist on everything being black or white, but is happy to play around with possibilities. One can imagine the Creator playing with an unimaginable number of possibilities: taking up some and letting others go, but finding delight in *all* possibilities.

To use our imagination in prayer is to open ourselves more widely to the wonder of God and to discern connections between things which show again and again the unity of creation, and show us more of how we belong to each other in Christ. We may find it hard at first to use our imagination, but it is worth persevering. For some it may never be the main path of prayer, but a kind of auxiliary, occasional path.

Some people will find it possible to go back imaginatively again and again to the Bible stories, which become much-loved friends, scenes which become richer with every renewed visit; for others, familiarity breeds not contempt but dullness and dryness. For such people it may be better to start on imaginative prayer from our own experience or from our own world, and allow that experience to lead us to God.

(1) Personal symbols, prayer and meditation

The biblical writers always take it for granted that dreams and visionary events are significant and are among the main ways in which God communicates with human beings. The presupposition of these writers is that through such experiences the past is given significance, the present can be coped with and the future can be opened up. Entrenched attitudes are often challenged and people are enabled to change direction in their lives in a creative manner. A good example of this is found in Peter's dream recorded in Acts 10. Through this dream Peter discovers the false nature of a narrow interpretation of the significance of Jesus, i.e. that salvation is only for the Jews. He thus becomes instrumental in opening the doors of the church to non-Jews.

Let us now move on to a practical exercise. The exercise is in two parts. The first part is undertaken in private, the second in a small group of people who trust one another. The aim of the exercise is to provide the individual with space and a way of recognizing their personal symbols. The sharing with the group provides a means of interpreting the symbols and discovering where common symbols occur.

Part 1

Discover a place where you can be alone and undisturbed for half an hour.

Sit in a comfortable chair in an upright position, feet flat on the floor and hands resting in your lap.

Acknowledge the sounds around you so that they do not intrude.

Breathe deeply, repeating in rhythm with your breathing some chosen words, e.g. 'Be still and know that I am God' or perhaps, 'Jesus, Son of Mary, Son of God, have mercy.' Continue this for as long as it takes for you to become physically and mentally relaxed.

Concentrate on the images which enter your mind. If a vivid mental picture unfolds itself, remember it in detail.

At the end of half an hour write down the details of your mental picture. (This method is also a very helpful way of working with dreams.)

Part 2

On a separate occasion, reflect further on the contents of these meditation images (and dream images). This can be undertaken alone but it can also be done with great profit in a small group.

When the group meets, share your images with each other. See where common symbols occur.

Reflect on the possible relevance of these to our shared human existence.

Help each other to explore the personal pictures. Try to help one another to relate the personal images to the pressures, problems, decisions and events of life. They may have a lot to tell you about your hopes and fears, your hurts and emotional scars, your perception of God and how God relates to you.

---

(2) Remembering

This is a simple exercise. After a period of quietening down in some appropriate way take your mind back to an early experience, not one you have been told about but one you can remember, for example:

the earliest experience of justice you can remember . . .

the earliest experience of injustice you can remember . . .
the first time you were aware of prayer . . .
the first time you really felt yourself to be loved . . .
the first time you were aware of Jesus . . .
the first time . . .

---

(3) Storytelling

Stories are nowadays being recovered as a wonderful way of shedding a new light on old Christian wisdom and truth. After a period of centring down, read this story through slowly, to yourself. Pause, when you have finished reading, before continuing with the exercise.

This story is a retelling of a legend about Lao Tzu, an ancient and revered Chinese teacher.

Once in the village of Zhang which lay at the foot of a tall mountain, the people were terrorized by a rampaging and marauding lion. Having suffered the loss of sheep and goats and fearing for the safety of their children, the villagers organized a hunting party to search out and destroy the beast. However, when their hunting party was unsuccessful they decided to consult with their teacher, Lao Tzu, who lived in the heavens and visited them in his bright chariot.

Lao Tzu listened carefully as they told their story and begged him to help them capture the lion. Lao Tzu replied, 'The real trouble is that you don't understand this mountain lion. I will help you, but I will need someone to go with me and we must take a small kid.' A youth and a young girl, Yung and Li Chi, stepped forward to accompany Lao Tzu, and a local goat farmer brought forth a small animal for them to use to trap the beast.

Lao Tzu and his companions approached the lion's cave and found the bones of dead animals scattered

45

about. At the rear of the cave they saw a mound of soft sand and Lao Tzu indicated that the kid should be placed there. As he did so the young man felt sorry for the small creature who would be devoured by the beast and the girl felt quite angry, but the kid curled up and went to sleep. 'Let us hide behind the rocks and wait for the lion to return,' said Lao Tzu.

After some time the beast did return, carrying a dead deer in his jaws. But, seeing the kid, he laid down the kill, approached the sleeping animal and began licking it with his tongue; the two animals rolled over each other, nestled in together and went back to sleep. And Lao Tzu and his two companions, wearied with the long wait, did so too!

When they awoke, the lion and the kid were gone. 'We've lost the kill,' objected Yung and Li Chi. 'The kill!' exclaimed Lao Tzu. 'Come and look.' And over the grassy knoll the lion could be seen lying in the sun seeming to watch as a mother over her child as the kid grazed. 'All is well,' said Lao Tzu. 'An innocent kid has tamed the ferocious lion; savage instincts have been replaced by love and gentleness. Let us return; I will come again in six months.'

Lao Tzu's companions were afraid the villagers would not believe their story but a few weeks later a woman washing in the stream was threatened by a poisonous serpent and at the last moment a creature, half lion and half human, came from the brush and saved her. Several other reports of this wondrous beast were given and Yung and Li Chi felt sure it was the transformed mountain lion.

Each story was repeated to Lao Tzu when he returned six months later. 'All is indeed well now,' he said. 'There is no need to fear the mountain lion who has been transformed by the power of love working in your midst.' As they were speaking a tall, attractive person came out of the woods and *all* felt certain it was the transformed mountain lion; the newcomer greeted Lao Tzu and the two went off in the bright chariot.

Surely we are all familiar with the many times when the small *is* actually swallowed by the stronger but in our own lives there will have been times when God has placed something on the pile of sand in the back of our caves . . . when in the middle of a beastly experience we have been aware of something, or someone, who distracted our thoughts or caught our attention . . . and because of this intervention we have been eased or soothed or enabled to feel more human. See if you can remember one such event now; bring it to mind and retell the story to yourself.

Allow a few minutes silence.

46

In the next period of silence, focus in turn on three elements from this story from your experience: each is a gift to you, so hold one at a time in your thoughts long enough to draw from each all the sweetness it has to offer you.

Focus first on yourself . . . where you were . . . what you were doing . . . how you felt. . . .

Secondly, focus on the person or object which came to you . . . how it looked . . . what it did . . . how you felt about it. . . .

Thirdly, recall the result.

Just before you release each element choose and remember one or two words. At the end of your reflection combine these words into a one-line statement of gratitude which will hold the experience and enable you to return to it in the future. For example: (1) despair, depression; (2) cowslip bloomed unexpectedly; (3) felt better. Put together these might become: 'Thank you God for my despair and the cowslip which eased it.'

○ (4) 'Except you become as little children . . .'

In the Gospels Jesus warns us that we lose touch with our playful child-bit at our peril. The following exercise may help to KEEP us in touch with the child within us, but also, perhaps, to GET us in touch with some other bits of ourselves and place both in relationship with God and with others.

Materials needed

A selection of small soft animal toys, enough for each member of the group with some left over so there can be a choice, and enough small candles or nightlights for every member.

Procedure

- Produce animals one by one from a box, briefly introducing some of them in a light-hearted way with a single sentence or so.
- Invite group members to choose a soft toy and ask them to sit by themselves (away from the group if they wish) and for about 15 minutes to imagine their animal's story.

47

– At the end of this period members go into twos for about 10 minutes to share their stories.

– The leader then explains that quite often we may find ourselves putting on to an animal (toy or real) bits of ourselves which we may find it hard to own for ourselves. These may be positive, good things about us, or they may be sad or even painful things in our lives, or qualities we would rather push away, pretending they are not there. Invite the group to think about this individually and to be ready to stay with and perhaps struggle with the harder bits rather than dismissing them or feeling guilty about them. (About 10 minutes)

Invite each member, in turn, to place their animal on the floor in the centre, or on a low table, and pause for a moment to pray silently for the story the animal has suggested, which will, of course, be partly their own story.

– Secondly, ask them to think of other people suggested to them by their story for whom they might like to pray. (10 minutes should be about right for this.)

– Then give each member a candle, and having lighted the candles ask for them to be placed in turn on a central low table, and for each person to pray aloud briefly for the people who have come to mind for them in the silence. If anyone is uneasy about praying aloud they may, of course, make their candle offering in silence.

– General discussion now follows on how the whole exercise felt for the group, concluding with a suitable prayer.

Postscript

Do not be surprised if some members ask to borrow their animal for a while in order to continue unfinished business! It does not require a great deal of imagination to put this exercise into the context of an informal house communion, with the bringing up of the toys at the offertory. A useful reading would be a condensation of the first half of *The Velveteen Rabbit* (Margery Williams, Little Mammoth publishers 1989).

○ (5) Vision of a healed world

This exercise may be used as an introductory exercise to learn about each other. It may also be used with an ongoing group to pray for the world. Young people may find it particularly useful.

Sit in a circle. Ask members of the group to imagine that they come from another planet (this gives freer rein to the imagination). On that planet is something special that allows for healing, e.g. silver sand – when it runs through your fingers all the children sing; or trees with blue leaves that when looked at make people forget their differences.

Allow a few minutes thinking time for people to decide what healing property is on their planet. Then go round the circle, starting with the leader, and say: 'I come from another planet, and on that planet there is. . . .'

By the time everyone has spoken the group will have learned not only something about each other, but also something of their vision of a healed world.

Next invite each member of the group to consider what are the healing properties of our world. Share this with the group.

This leads into a period of prayer for all the woundedness of the world, and perhaps especially of the inner city.

49

○ (6) Dying/letting go

This is a powerful exercise and might be best done as a group exercise. If so, the sections can be spoken by the leader, or perhaps, since we all need different amounts of time, a handout might be better so that members of the group can move at their own pace. Allow plenty of time for discussion at the end as deep and maybe difficult feelings may have arisen.

Brief silence, eyes closed and relaxed.

Time for relaxation.

Begin to imagine your own death.

How old are you?

Where are you?

What are you dying from?

Are you alone or is there someone with you?

If so, who *is* with you, or who do you *want* to be with you?

What do you *want* to say to them, and what *are* your last words to them?

What are their last words to you?

What is happening just before and just after your death?

Is there any sense of the presence of good or evil?

What are your feelings?
    Alone?   Happy?
    Afraid?   Glad?
    Angry?   Peaceful?
    Sad?

Coming out of the exercise
What do you feel now that you are not dying?

Short silence.

Are there any other minor experiences of letting go that are better understood now in the light of that exercise, e.g. moving house, children leaving home, changing job?

Does thinking about our own mortality in any way equip us for living?

Those who are led by the Holy Spirit see clearly. That is why so many of the ignorant know more than the wise.

CURÉ D'ARS

5
Adoration and Contemplation

You yourself are even another little world and have within you the sun and the moon and also the stars.

ORIGEN

Introduction

There is much confusion about terminology. Often people use the word 'meditation' when they really mean 'contemplation', while the Ignatian tradition uses the word 'contemplation' when referring to what others call 'meditation'!

By 'meditation' (sometimes 'discursive meditation') we will be referring to the active use of the mind, the feelings, the imagination, applied to a passage of Scripture, or our own situation in life, or to any active way in which we try to understand God or ourselves in relation to God or God's world. This activity *brings in* a great richness and may well lead us to the expression of joy or wonder, thanksgiving, penitence or intercession. *Bringing in* rather than excluding.

Contemplative prayer is in some senses almost the opposite. Some temperaments, or some people at a certain stage of their life, come to find that the ideas, the images, the imagination, the feelings, good though they are, somehow *get in the way* between God and themselves. They wish to be open to God *as he is* without anything getting in the way. So in contemplative prayer we shall try to put aside all the interesting thoughts and ideas that come to us, and simply home in on a single word or phrase or symbol.

This is not a question of self-hypnosis. It is not trying to imagine we are having lovely feelings. After the first few months of practising contemplative prayer we are more likely to find ourselves in a desert of blankness, wondering whether there is any point in what we are doing, and yet still unable to let go of something to which we believe we have been called.

We are simply waiting upon God, being open to God, being available for God, longing towards God in a kind of inner darkness, which though dark is nevertheless friendly.

Contemplative prayer is not for everyone, and those for whom it is not helpful should never feel they are somehow second class in the work of prayer. In the same way those who genuinely do not find Bible meditation helpful must never be made to feel that they 'ought' to be able to do it. Our enthusiasms all too often carry us away and lead to a lack of sensitivity to the fact that others may be coming from a different place. It is a question of temperament, and to find the right way of prayer for us at any given time is far more important than trying to pursue a current fashion.

It follows, therefore, that while most prayer groups will probably want to explore contemplative prayer from time to time (a simple method is offered in the last exercise in this chapter), a prayer group which is specifically contemplative (or for that matter always doing Bible meditations) will need to be selective in its membership.

Having said all that, it remains a fact that simple contemplative prayer is helpful to many more people than used to be thought. If we are taking it really seriously we shall be wise either to have a spiritual director we can talk to, or belong to a contemplative prayer group where we can share with others, because we can sometimes find ourselves in quite deep water and may feel bewildered.

---

(1) Listening prayer

This exercise falls into three parts.

Concentration

(a) It may be helpful to use a cross, a candle, a flower, or some other 'focus'.

(b) Breathe in slowly, praying, 'Fill me, Holy Spirit.' Breathe out, praying, 'Cleanse me from my sin.' Do this several times.

(c) Acknowledge how you are feeling physically. Take note of any pain, irritation or discomfort. Notice the sounds around you. Acknowledge the thoughts in your mind – anxieties, things to remember, feelings of well-being or anticipation.

(d) Clench your hands, fingers downwards. Put into words (silently) the thoughts and concerns uppermost in your mind – a decision to be made, someone who is in trouble, a sick friend or relative, a difficult marriage relationship, etc. There's no need to go into detail – God already knows.

(e) Now lay these thoughts and cares, one by one, before God, and *let them go*.

Drop them by opening your hands, palms down. It may require an effort – wipe your hands together if you need to, or shake them.

Reflection

(a) Spend some time looking back; perhaps at a recent encounter with a friend, perhaps at the events of the day or the week; try to limit yourself to two or three incidents.

(b) Reflect on your behaviour – be honest! Are there things you regret? Things you shouldn't have said? Things you feel you did well?

(c) Allow yourself to be led to repentance; to intercession; or to thanksgiving – share it with God.

(d) As you relate your behaviour and feelings in prayer allow yourself to become aware of God's forgiveness, his compassion, his delight in *you*.

Attention*

(a) Be conscious of the nearness of God – in the breath you are breathing, in your silence. He has heard your prayer.

(b) Rest quietly in his presence; enjoy simply loving him; enjoy the wonder of his love for you, his interest and concern for all that matters to you; his loving acceptance of all you are and will become.

(c) Finally, recall those things which you earlier laid at his feet. Open your hands, palms up, and receive them again, one by one, transformed and transfigured in his presence and love. And go on your way rejoicing!

---

* If time is short or a particular problem needs to be prayed over, use the first section (a) and then the final section (c).

---

(2) Adoration: an exercise in coming to God as we are

The following exercise may initially appear a little complicated, but it's really very straightforward and very helpful!

One of the barriers to the prayer of adoration or of contemplation is an inability to face up to ourselves, our pain or our anxiety. The following could be used with a group in an attempt to help people learn that it is safe to come to God as they are, and that he can cope with them and *all* their feelings.

Materials needed

Paper and pencils, two large sheets of paper and felt-tip pens. Bibles should be available.

The exercise includes a period of silent prayer, and it is helpful if the

meeting is held in a place where people can have some freedom, e.g. by going into church or a quiet room, for a walk, etc.

It is important that the leader and at least one other are available to be consulted if needed during the quiet time (d).

(a) Begin by writing the word GOD on one of the large papers. Ask the group to think for a few minutes in silence, and in the silence to jot down the words that come into their minds when they think about God. Then ask them to share their thoughts in pairs for five minutes or so. Next, ask the group to read out the words and write them up on the large sheet of paper and allow some time to discuss these images and epithets of God.

(b) Then write ME on the other large piece of paper, following the procedure as above, but emphasizing that when it comes to sharing and discussion no one should feel pressured to reveal anything they do not feel comfortable to share, though they may find it helpful to jot it down for their own use.

(c) There now follows a discussion on the contrast between the two sets of words. How did the group members feel about this contrast? Did they feel unworthy or inadequate in God's presence? Was this a barrier to prayer? Were they afraid of coming to God? Were they fearful of the pain, anguish, anger, etc. they might experience in silence? The ultimate purpose of this discussion is to encourage members of the group to lay hold of the belief that God accepts them as they are; that in the incarnation God showed confidence in human beings, despite their frailty. There is a wealth of biblical material and wisdom from the tradition and personal experience that the leader can feed in from his or her own 'treasures'.

If the 'God words' emphasize transcendence and righteousness, it will be important to balance them with concepts of immanence (the closeness of God), of 'Abba', Father, of 'loving-kindness', of acceptance and confidence (Zacchaeus, the woman at the well of Samaria), of the feminine in God as described by Mother Julian, and so on.

(d) After the discussion, encourage group members to go and pray for about twenty minutes, bringing what lay behind their ME words into God's presence, with the trust that they are accepted as they are. Encourage them to do this where and how they like. Discourage them, however, from reading, except perhaps the Bible, but suggest they do not try to force things if they find them too difficult or too long. They may talk to the leader or another person if necessary.

(e) The session ends with a discussion on how people got on and on how this way of praying might be helpful in other areas of life (e.g. self-acceptance, enabling acceptance of others).

It is important to give the exercise a light and natural touch. It should not be a time of self-agonizing, but rather one of confident self-acceptance. Humour helps, as well as the realization that the leader has 'been there before'.

○ **(3)   A meeting for worship after the manner of Friends**

The following has been contributed by a Quaker. As it stands it is not a clear-cut prayer exercise, but it provides ample information to enable a group leader to run a prayer group 'for a meeting for worship after the manner of Friends', and may encourage further reading about this important Christian tradition. A simple way would be to read the passage below and then move into a one-hour 'Quaker meeting'.

The seventeenth century was a time when many were questioning the beliefs and religious practices of the age. One such young man, George Fox, after seeking the advice of many priests and 'professors' and finding none who could speak to his condition, then had a transforming religious experience of the presence of Christ.

Fox went on to preach that 'Christ is come to teach his people himself', that he is present to those who seek and listen to him, that he gives us the power to do what is right, that he brings his people into fellowship and helps them to endure adversity if they are faithful. When this gospel was preached, those who received it came together to worship and to wait for their teacher – the Inward Christ – to speak to them. This is the origin of the Quaker meeting.

Friends believe that 'the light within' is not an abstract phrase but an experience, that the light is present and everyone can, if he or she wishes, have a living experience of God within. The light is not divided, but the same light is in all and is a force for unity; we can therefore test our leadings in community.

It is in silence that we come closest to God. The silent meeting is not an end in itself, but the silence leads us into stillness and the stillness leads to an awareness of the presence of God. As the late Rufus Jones wrote:

> The early Friends made the discovery that silence is one of the best preparations for communion with God and for the reception of inspiration and guidance. Silence itself has no magic. It may be just sheer emptiness, absence of words or noise of music. It may be an occasion for slumber, or it may be a dead form. But it may also be an intensified pause, a vitalized hush,

a creative quiet, an actual moment of mutual and reciprocal correspondence with God. The actual meeting of man with God and God with man is the very crown and culmination of what we can do with our human life here on earth.

Friends use the term 'gathered meeting' to describe times when those present are gathered, in the sense of being drawn into a common centre. The presence is felt and the silence takes on a new quality.

Out of this silence a Friend may be moved to stand and speak. The word 'moved' is used literally, for many Friends experience a pounding of the heart (quite unlike stage fright), and often other physical symptoms which come upon them if they are given ministry to offer.

Ministry should arise, as Friends say, out of the exercise of the meeting. We do not come to the meeting determined to speak (or not to speak). Certainly we should by devotional reading, prayer, or meditation prepare ourselves through the week but we should only speak if we are moved to do so. Spoken ministry should arise out of the silence and lead back into it. This is not a time for debate, discussion or critical analysis. Thoughts may come which are not for sharing. They may be for oneself alone or may even be the seed of ministry which may appropriately be spoken on some future occasion.

The ministry of one may become the seed for the meditation of another. If this happens, he or she may in turn be moved to speak so that a common theme is developed that grips the mind of all those present and they find themselves drawn into a unity in which the presence of the spirit of God is realized. At its best, the meeting for worship will justify the claim, in humility, that Christ's real presence is known when two or three are gathered together in quiet expectancy.

These days, Quaker meetings for worship are usually closed, after one hour, by an elder shaking hands with one seated nearby, which gesture is taken up by others. But an elder, who is sensitive to the life of the Spirit in the meeting, may either close it sooner or let it run on for a while if either course is appropriate.

Vocal ministry is not essential to a meeting; the sense of the presence in the midst may well be found in a meeting which remains completely silent. However, if a meeting is habitually silent, something may be missing in the corporate relationship.

---

(4) Towards contemplation

Please begin by reading the introduction to this chapter before planning your session.

(a) Begin with a simple awareness or relaxation exercise, and/or a breathing exercise.

(b) Silently recollect and then *let go* of all the things which are worrying or burdening you in your own life or in the lives of those near to you. Recollect and let go. We might imagine we are taking off a very heavy rucksack and putting it down for God to look after for a space. Offer the words to be repeated silently, 'Come to me all you who labour and are heavy laden and I will give you rest' (shortening to 'Come to me and I will give you rest'). Be brief and businesslike; this is not the heart of the work, this is simply clearing out what gets in the way between God and us for, say, two or three minutes.

(c) We now take a simple phrase and hold it in the mind, in the heart, in the will. Let's take an attribute of God – PEACE: 'My peace I give you, not as the world gives do I give you' (shorten to 'My peace I give you' or simply 'My peace'). Whenever our minds wander we come back to the watchword. Through the indwelling Holy Spirit that divine peace is already potentially within us and we are simply trying to be open to that peace, not in any sense of trying to induce lovely

peaceful feelings, but in order that we shall *be* more peaceful people in the world, that we shall be able to express something of God's peace in our lives. If we do have a deep sensation of peace then we may thank God for it, but the purpose of contemplative prayer is not to cultivate feelings; the purpose is to allow ourselves to be conformed more closely to the likeness of Christ.

It is important for people to realize it is likely that nothing will 'happen'; rather we are placing ourselves as completely as we can for the time being at God's disposal in a longing towards that which we know only dimly.

(d) Intercession is not as far from contemplation as is sometimes thought; in interceding we bring another person into our contemplation of God to share in the sunlight, as it were. Christians cannot keep good things to themselves and a contemplative prayer time may well find a gentle inward pressure to end with a period of intercessory prayer.

Other suggested watchwords:

'These things I have spoken to you that my joy may be in you and your joy complete' (shorten to 'My joy in you' or 'My joy').

'Dwell in my love, for apart from me you can do nothing' (shorten to 'Dwell in my love').

'Whoever finds me finds life.'

'All power is given to me in heaven and on earth, and I am with you always' (shorten to 'All power is given to me' – but remember that divine power is frequently manifested in weakness).

Contemplation can, of course, also concentrate on the visual – a tree, a flower, a bowl of water, a seed . . . remember Dame Julian's hazelnut!

(e) You may like to round off the exercise with a suitable prayer. Robert Coulson, founder of the Fellowship of Contemplative Prayer, always ended prayer sessions with a prayer which ran roughly as follows:

We thank you, Lord, that you have heard us and we offer to you, as far as we are able, as an emptiness to be filled with your peace [or joy or love], which flows ceaselessly from you, as rays from the sun, we offer to you, as far as we are able, all that we are, all that we have, and all that we hope for.

He who looks outwardly, dreams; he who looks within, awakes.

CARL JUNG

6
Prayer in Liturgy

Come, let us go up to the mountain of the Lord, to the house of the God of Jacob; that he may teach us his ways, and that we may walk in his paths.

ISAIAH 2.3 (RSV)

Introduction

It is surprisingly easy to forget, in a book of prayer exercises, the value that has been and undoubtedly still is found in the use of orders of service. After all, most people's first experience of prayer is in the context of an order of service in a church.

The practice of saying prayers at particular hours of the day or night was general among the Jews, and seems to have been taken over by the early Christians (cf. Acts 2.46; 3.1; 10.9, 30; 16.25). In time there developed a pattern of eight times of prayer (or offices) in monastic use, and the arrangement was worked out in some detail by St Benedict. At the Reformation the Church of England reshaped the pattern to give the two offices of Morning and Evening Prayer (Mattins and Evensong).

Not all Christians find set prayers helpful, but for many they can offer a shape to a day or a week, becoming a 'comfortable peg' that consecrates time.

Most services (or offices) are readily adaptable for use by an individual or by a small group meeting in someone's home. The exercises offered in this chapter are no more than a taste of the possibilities that are available. The first encourages a group to produce an order of service of its own. The second allows people to experience the different flavour of modern as compared to traditional language, while the third looks at a familiar service in a rather different way.

(1)   Create an office

General preparation for the exercise:

Write a list of what you'd like to see in a common prayer.

Are you looking for: Adoration?
                       Confession?
                       Thanksgiving?
                       Intercession?

Are you looking for components such as:
    Reading of sacred writings/Psalms etc.?
    Hymns?
    Silence?
    Prayers (what kind)?
    Speech/song/music?
    What about the use of the senses?
    What about the use of movement? etc.

When you've produced the office, pray it.

On the other hand, you may just like to produce a booklet that has a little prayer that could be used at different points in the day and make use of external factors such as news broadcasts (springboard for intercession), BBC Radio 4's 'Thought for the Day' or similar (an aid to meditation), habits such as washing (symbolic of baptism – a fresh start/confession etc.). Jewish people have set prayers for every time of day to help them to be more attentive to God's presence at a particular moment.

(2)   Compline

The debate about modern and traditional language seems to persist – in worship, in our preference for a particular translation of the Bible over others, and indeed in our prayers.

On the one hand modern language can give clarity of expression, freshness of new images, and reinterpretation – going beyond narrow translation. On the other hand, traditional language has the advantages of deep familiarity, and a valuable peculiarity, hinting at otherness.

This exercise is intended to help you explore the advantages of both.

First, say the office of Compline (in traditional form; published in pamphlet form by SPCK). Then keep a longish silence, as seems appropriate. Say a modern night-time service such as 'Prayer at Night*. Conclude with a time for gentle reflection on the alternative forms.

Note: It would be possible to use a service other than Compline, perhaps Mattins or Evensong.

*Compiled by Jim Cotter, available from Cairns Publications, 47, Firth Park Avenue, Sheffield S5 6NF.

◯ (3) The silent Eucharist

A Eucharist celebrated in silence may seem to be a contradiction. Possibly it is! Nevertheless, many who have tried it out have found the silence to be **very** rich and have discovered new insights in God's action at the Eucharist. Almost certainly it needs to be used only with people who are familiar with the shape of the Eucharist.

At the end of this section there is a brief rationale and plan for a silent Eucharist and it is suggested that something similar should be copied and given to everyone taking part. Careful thought must be given as to how the essential movement of eucharistic worship can be best expressed. Manual acts by the President should be carefully considered (and kept simple).

There is no blueprint. What is offered here is reflection on experience of such services and an example of one such service. If you wish to plan such a service you will need to do your own work and use your own imagination. You will also need to be very tightly organized, having thought through clearly what people will need to be given before the service starts.

Suggestions (but there are all sorts of possibilities):

(a) Worship space. Table, icon, candle . . . people arranged in a circle. Chairs for comfort.

(b) Let people ask questions about what is going to happen. Give clear instructions about any movement or action required and try to help people feel comfortable and secure. Silence can be very frightening.

(c) Consider using a piece of music as a call to worship and to lead into the silence.

(d) Confession. Pieces of paper given out by the President can be written on, folded and placed in a suitable container. These may then be burnt or torn up by the President.

(e) Gospel. If there is time, prepare a mime for one or more people. If not, someone can be appointed to move to the centre of the circle, hold an open Bible for a short period, possibly lifting it slightly before sitting down.

(f) Intercession. Each person can come forward and light a candle as they offer their intercession in silence.

(g) Peace. Begun by the President. Others may follow his actions at this point, a handshake or an embrace. (We found it very difficult to remain silent!)

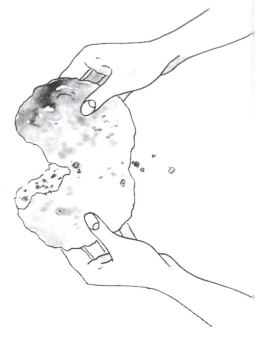

(h) Eucharistic Prayer and beyond. The President's actions must give full expression to the fourfold action here:

 – Taking the bread and cup
 – Giving thanks over the bread and cup.

– Breaking the bread.
– Giving the bread and cup to the assembled worshippers, possibly encouraging them to administer to each other in the round.

The material printed below was given at a silent Eucharist of the Holy Spirit celebrated at a SPIDIR training course meeting. Classical music was thought to be most helpful on this occasion and for this particular group, but many different styles of music would be suitable, e.g. 'Eat this bread' from the community at Taizé could be used at the communion or as an invitation to communion.

A possible order

At the celebration of the Eucharist we are usually expected to respond physically with body and voice. Today we are released from these expectations and invited to use the freedom given to allow ourselves to be more open to the promptings of the Spirit.

The liturgy will follow the usual eucharistic shape, which is set out below for those who find it useful.

Call to worship ('Locus iste' – Anton Bruckner. 'This place was made by God a priceless mystery; it is without reproof.')

Confession and Absolution.

Collect: Come now, spirit of integrity, of tenderness, judgement, and dance; touch our speechlessness, kindle our longing, reach into our silence, and fire our words with your truth; that each may hear in her own language the mighty works of God.

Gospel: John 14.25–7 (JB)

Jesus said: 'I have said these things to you while still with you; but the Advocate, the Holy Spirit, whom the Father will send in my name, will teach you everything and remind you of all I have said to you.
'Peace I bequeath to you, my own peace I give you, a peace the world cannot give, this is my gift to you. Do not let your hearts be troubled or afraid.'

After the Gospel: an excerpt from *The Kingdom* by Edward Elgar will be played.

Intercession
Peace
Eucharistic Prayer
Lord's Prayer
Breaking of Bread
Invitation to communion
Communion
Blessing
Dismissal

Beasts and all cattle; creeping things, and flying fowl . . . praise the Lord.

PSALM 148

7
Prayer and Reconciliation

True penitence must be God-centred and not self-centred: self-disgust keeps us in ourselves, while penitence gives hope – the difference between Judas and Peter in their differing reactions. One leads to despair, but penitence tries to make up for the harm done to others, and is not self-concerned.

ANON

Introduction

At the heart of the Christian message is reconciliation, which means recognizing our sinfulness and taking steps to restore unity lost through sin by becoming once again at one with ourselves, with our neighbours, with the whole creation and with God. Reconciliation has its source in God and for us to receive this free gift we need to give ourselves space to take a look at ourselves and offer our lives afresh to God. For the Christian, Jesus – the sinless one – is the model and objective external measure of what it means to be in unity and reconciled and so he is the focus of our hope.

The Church through sacraments offers reconciliation, be it through the Eucharist or through baptism which may be seen as the foundation sacraments of reconciliation. In the early church it was stressed that baptism was a complete break with the old life (Rom. 6.6) and sin thereafter was seen as having no part in the life of the new community. That is why the sin of Ananias and Sapphira (Acts 5.1-11) was seen as so awful. Initially there appears to have been little opportunity in the Church for reconciliation after a fall, though a one-off form of public confession of sin seems to have been allowed after a long period of exclusion from the fellowship. This was known as exomologesis. In Britain it was the Celtic monks in later centuries who made reconciliation a much more private affair with the confession of sins to a pastor/priest of a community and the offering of the assurance of forgiveness. By the time of the Fourth Lateran Council in 1215 the practice of exomologesis was completely ousted and replaced by private confession. Since that time penitential rites have tended to focus upon the failings of the individual. In most cases they proceed from an examination of the individual conscience (often in the past prompted by 'check lists' of possible sins) through an act of contrition and confession towards the hearing of God's forgiveness in the absolution (possibly accompanied by an act of penance) and consequent thanksgiving.

Today the ministry of reconciliation is being rediscovered by many Christian traditions and taken out of the sphere of, on the one hand, a purely private prayer between 'me and God' and on the other, the practice of a rather overgeneral confession contained in the liturgy. The exercises offered below help us to explore some of the middle ground between the private and the general forms of reconciliation.

---

(1) Forgiven and free

Peace with God

Read Micah 7.19.

Read 1 John 2.1-2.

God does not want us to be burdened by guilt. He wants to free us and pour out his forgiveness on us. It is a gift we cannot earn and as a gift it is to be received with open and empty hands.

Read Psalm 139.23-4.

God examine me and know my heart, probe me and know my thoughts; make sure I do not follow pernicious ways, and guide me in the way that is everlasting.

Ask the Holy Spirit to show you if there is any sin in your life that he would like you to confess. Spend about one minute in silence listening to God before going on to the next step.

It may help to picture Jesus cn the cross in your mind's eye.

Hear his words to you, 'Friend, your sins are forgiven' (Luke 5.20).

With open hands receive the forgiveness he offers and thank him.

Peace with others

Forgiving others involves an act of will, the making of a choice on our part. Sometimes, we can do no more than make a beginning; it may take time before our feelings follow on. We need God's help. We need to be honest with God about how we feel and to bring those feelings to the cross. If you do not yet feel ready to forgive, ask God to help. 'I wish I wanted to forgive' may be a place to begin a prayer which echoes that of the Father of the child with epilepsy in Mark 9.25 ('I do have faith. Help the little faith I have'). Forgiving a person is not the same as condoning what they have done, accepting their views or being manipulated by them.

Read Colossians 3.13.

Bear with one another; forgive each other as soon as a quarrel begins. The Lord has forgiven you; now you must do the same.

Ask the Holy Spirit to show you if there is anyone you need to forgive. This may include yourself or someone who has not asked your forgiveness. You might need to ask God's forgiveness for the mistaken view you have had of him or her.

Do you want to forgive?

Ask God to help you to release that person.

Peace in the world

Is there a situation you know of where forgiveness and reconciliation would be appropriate between the people involved in broken relationships?

Two people?
Within a family?
Within a church?
Groups in conflict within a nation?
Conflict between nations?

Where is God in this situation and what does he want for those people?

End the time together with a suitable prayer or by everyone saying the Lord's Prayer and the Grace.

If you have found any of these sections difficult, find someone whom you trust to talk it over with.

(2) Forgiveness

I shall remove the heart of stone . . . and give you a heart of flesh (Ezek. 36.26 REB).

To tackle our failings may be quite painful. Posture, too, might be noted; if we are considering forgiveness it might be helpful to emphasize the activity by kneeling.

A painting of the crucifixion or a crucifix will give a focus to the prayer, as we kneel before the cross.

So kneeling at the foot of the cross talk silently to Christ on the cross about your need for forgiveness, or the struggle you are having to forgive or to be reconciled, and allow our Lord to talk back to you about it.

Or, still kneeling there, being present to the cross, allow the hardness, the bitterness, the anger, the resentment which you find welling up inside yourself and knotting you up, to flow out of you onto that figure on the cross, and to feel love flowing back from him, cleansing and forgiving.

Sometimes people need to be reconciled with a particular person or with a group of people, in which case they can imagine themselves standing or kneeling at the foot of that cross with those people and allowing the aggression to flow onto Christ on the cross, and again to feel his love flowing into them and being drawn to them.

A very simple alternative exercise in forgiveness, also suitable for use in retreats, and especially for married people, is to go out of doors and find for yourself a stone which will represent to you something which you want to give up, like anger, bitterness, or resentment. Again you kneel either in imagination at the foot of the cross, or before the painting, clutching the stone with its symbolism. You are likely to hold it in your fists as though it were your last treasure, but when eventually you feel you can, you go to the cross and place the stone there at its foot.

───────

○ (3) Reconciliation and Fire

The following prayer exercises are offered for use during occasions when we wish to make a special emphasis on forgiveness. Two alternative approaches are given, but both are essentially liturgical – one drawing its inspiration from Ash Wednesday, the other drawing its inspiration from Maundy Thursday. The exercises assume the presence of a priest, but may be adapted for lay use.

(Please ensure that there are no smoke detectors in the vicinity, and if there are, temporarily remove the batteries.)

Materials required

Firelighters
Bowl for fire (brazier)
Charcoal
Matches
Paper
Pencil
Books to lean on

It is essential to make sure that the fire is entirely safe and won't burn the place down. Raise the brazier on bricks and don't put so much fuel in that you get sparks everywhere. If in doubt have the fire outside and look at it through a french window.

General Introduction

The general tone should be set that we are exploring a return to God and reconciliation with each other. 'Come back with all your heart', not with a great show, but inwardly in the secret place of your heart, by not neglecting the grace we have received. The emphasis might be on the joyful aspect of repentance – the return of the prodigal son being a powerful picture of this (Luke 15.11–32).

74

A hymn with a confessional quality to it may be sung, e.g. 'Kyrie eleison' (no. 92 in *Cry Hosanna*, ed. Betty Pulkingham and Mimi Farra, Hodder & Stoughton 1980) or 'Per Crucem' (p. 109 in *Music from Taizé*, Jacques Berthier, Collins 1982).

Opening Prayer

Let us pray
(extemporize particular concerns)
Lord,
protect us in the struggle against evil as we come before you seeking to be reconciled with you,
ourselves, our neighbour and creation.
We ask this through our Lord Jesus Christ who lives and reigns with you and the Holy Spirit ever one God world without end. Amen.

Some possible readings:
Joel 2.12–18
2 Cor. 5.20—6.2
Matt. 6.1–6, 16–18.

Confession

My sisters and brothers, God calls us to conversion; let us therefore ask him for the grace of sincere repentance.

Lord, send your Spirit among us
to cleanse us with the fire of your Spirit.
May he make of us a living sacrifice
so that in every place
we may praise your glory
and proclaim your loving compassion.
We ask this through Christ our Lord. Amen.

Music and words follow (some suggestions follow) to help people write down on paper their sins – (anything that they feel causes a division between themselves and God). No one will see them! At the end of the period allowed for confession a fire is lit and people are invited to put their confessions in the flames as a symbol of how God utterly blots out their sins.

Any form of appropriate words may be used during the Confession – the Beatitudes (Matt. 5.1–12) being one example. Another form is given below:

Jesus teaches us to love the Lord our God with our whole heart and mind. So we ask that we may see ourselves as God sees us.

- Do I live for self, or for God?
- Do I try to do his will or my own?
- Do I pray regularly?
- What are the false gods in my heart, idols of money, etc?
- Have I used God's name in vain?

Jesus teaches us to love our neighbours as ourselves: in the light of his example we might ask ourselves:

- Do I want to know my neighbour, or am I content with a small circle of friends?
- Am I totally absorbed with my family to the extent of excluding others?
- Do I spend enough time with my family?
- Does my life reflect my vocation as a baptized Christian?
- Do I set a good example?

– Do I see my work as a service to others?

– Am I honest in my dealings with others?

– Am I aware and do I take due notice of my social responsibility?

– Am I concerned about justice and the needs of the poor?

– Do I care for the sick and the weak?

– Have I injured my neighbour by gossip?

– Am I willing to forgive those who have wronged me?

Jesus teaches us that we must strive to be perfect as our heavenly Father is perfect. We might therefore ask ourselves:

– Have I acted as my conscience suggests?

– Have I sinned against my own body with drink, overeating, etc.

– Am I proud and self-opinionated?

– Have I lied?

– Have I indulged in self-pity?

– Am I patient?

– Have I been lazy, apathetic or indifferent?

– Do I overwork?

God set us over creation as its steward.

– Am I wasteful of resources?

– Do I appreciate the created order?

– Do I use the gifts that God has given to me?

(The pieces of paper are put on the brazier.)

Concluding General Confession

I confess to almighty God,
and to you, my brothers and sisters,
that I have sinned through my own fault
in my thoughts and in my words,
in what I have done,
and in what I have failed to do;
and I ask you, my brothers and sisters,
in the communion of saints,
to pray for me to the Lord our God.

The Absolution (given by a priest if present)

God, the Father of mercies,
through the death and resurrection of his Son
has reconciled the world to himself
and sent the Holy Spirit among us
for the forgiveness of sins;
through the ministry of the Church
may God give you/us pardon and peace,
and absolve you/us from your sins
in the name of the Father, and of the Son,
and of the Holy Spirit. Amen.

People may prefer to come forward for an individual prayer of absolution from the priest.

A hymn giving thanks for God's forgiveness may be sung (e.g. 'God forgave my sin in Jesus' name', no. 60 in *Mission Praise*, Marshall, Morgan and Scott 1983).

○ (4) Reconciliation and Water

(As in the previous exercise, but using water instead of fire as the symbol of washing away our sins.)

Lord, send your Spirit among us
to cleanse us in the waters of repentance.
May he make of us a living sacrifice
so that in every place
we may praise your glory
and proclaim your loving compassion.
We ask this through Christ our Lord
Amen.

Some form of preparation for confession is used as suggested in the previous exercise, but it is suggested that sins are not written down on paper since there is no opportunity to destroy them. The Miserere might be played (Ps. 50 (51)) or a reading such as Ezek. 36.21–9.

At the end of the preparation the following gospel reading might be used: John 13.1–15.

During the gospel someone carries a bowl of water and assists everyone to wash their hands as a sign of washing away of sin. (The priest if vested removes his outer garment.)

If no priest is present then there might be a more mutual arrangement of washing each other's hands and a corporate request for God's forgiveness at the end.

The Absolution is given in an appropriate form. There are many suitable hymns and choruses that may be sung during the liturgy, including:

Guide me, O thou great redeemer
Rock of Ages
Come to the waters
(no. 37, *Mission Praise*)

○ (5) Corporate Penance

The objective

This prayer exercise is an attempt to respond to the need to examine the corporate dimension to our 'sinfulness' which requires some sort of mutual expression.

Leader's notes

There are some obvious difficulties in the enterprise of corporate penance. First, it may be necessary to spend a considerable amount of time on the examination of the corporate conscience. This requires an understanding that simply by living in a developed nation at the end of the twentieth century we are inextricably linked with so many of the problems, injustices and disasters of the little planet which we inhabit. Such an examination will reveal both areas of our individual lives over which we can and should exercise control in the interests of all the people of the earth, but also situations to which we can respond only with the heart.

The second difficulty is that whilst such an examination may lead to appropriate acts of contrition and confession, there is no absolution possible in the traditional sense. We cannot simply put aside our corporate involvement: it is bound to continue. There is therefore the danger of creating an unspecified general feeling of guilt which is probably not, of itself, very constructive. Set against that must be the need, as individuals, to consider how we might adapt our lifestyles in the light of these discoveries, but we should not then conclude that, having done 'our bit', the problems can be left to someone else. It is somewhere within this dilemma of massive corporate responsibility and minuscule individual response that the final act of prayer takes place.

The structure of the exercise

– Examination of the corporate conscience and its relation to the individual. (45 minutes approx.)
– A corporate act of contrition. (15 minutes)
– An offering of personal responsibility. (15 minutes)
– Watching with the crucified Christ. (15 minutes)

Examination of the corporate conscience

Your hands are covered in blood, wash, make yourselves clean.
Take your wrong-doing out of my sight.
Cease doing evil. Learn to do good, search for justice, help the oppressed,
be just to the orphan, plead for the widow. (Isa. 1.15b–17 JB)

The leader begins with a reading like this one from Isaiah and reminds the group of how an examination of conscience normally focuses upon matters of personal behaviour and morality in relation to those with whom we have day-to-day contact. We are then reminded that throughout Scripture God also demands corporate morality in terms of the care of the environment (e.g. Lev. 25.1–7), justice for the poor (e.g. Lev. 25.8–17) and peace between peoples (e.g. Matt. 5.9). In our own day the World Council of Churches has launched an initiative to remind us of these responsibilities under the title 'Justice, Peace and the Integrity of Creation'.

One way to move from the abstract to the concrete is by way of the news media, but this will probably require a degree of explanation. The leader chooses an item of current news (a newspaper report, magazine article, or even a video of a TV news clip) and attempts to examine how we are interlinked to events which seem to be far away and remote, for example news of yet another famine. The cause of such a famine may be complex but might include climatic change (which may be related to our pollution of the atmosphere . . . including driving cars, using electricity generated by fossil fuels, using CFC-powered aerosols), civil war (sustained by the continuation of the arms trade) plus years of failure to establish just trade relations which would give Third World producers a proper economic return for their produce.

Once the general principle is established, each member of the group is given a suitable resource such as a recent newspaper or news magazine and is given time to look for one story where the link between our own life and some failure of humanity seems apparent. Each group member is also supplied with a sheet of paper and has access to scissors, glue, felt-tip pens, etc., and is invited to illustrate how he or she understands that linkage in words/pictures/cuttings or collage.

The group is reconvened and members are invited to pin their illustrations onto a suitably large board and to say a few words of explanation.

A corporate act of contrition

Using the pinboard as a visual focus, the group is invited to express its sorrow at its participation in the pain, destruction and injustice which have been demonstrated.

Some corporate act is demanded at this point. It could take the form of a litany but perhaps an act which leads into silence is to be preferred. One way of achieving this is through the repetitive singing of a chant, e.g. 'Salvator mundi' (*Music from Taizé*, vol.1) which can be sung through a number of times, getting quieter until the sound dies away and the song is continued in the heart. Fifteen minutes could be devoted to this part of the exercise, most of which would be spent in silence. The silence can be concluded by the leader picking up the 'Salvator mundi' at an audible level once again. If the leader lacks confidence about sustaining the music, a tape-recording of the chant can be used and the group encouraged to join in.

A suitable alternative, if music is felt inappropriate, is the corporate repetition of the Jesus Prayer:

> Lord Jesus Christ, son of the living God,
> have mercy upon me, a sinner.

The prayer can, like the chant, begin audibly, die away into silence and be picked up again at the end of the allotted time.

An offering of personal responsibility

The exercise up to this point may engender feelings of guilt and the inevitable desire to take away the pain of culpability by 'doing something about it'. It may be necessary at this stage, therefore, to allow the expression of such feelings in open discussion. The conclusion of that discussion might include some of the following thoughts:

(i) The scale of the problems and the extent of their complexity are massive;

(ii) We cannot by our actions 'solve' any of them;

(iii) Nonetheless, by taking personal responsibility for some of the consequences of our actions we become important signs of the kingdom of God in our time:

'To live in today's world and within it offer the solitary witness of staying unentangled, uncompromised by its power-struggles, unviolated by its attempts to corrupt, is what will . . . change the world' (Maggie Ross, *Pillars of Flame*, SCM Press 1988).

Each member of the group is then asked to think about *one* of the illustrations on the pinboard (not necessarily their own) and to consider *one* element of their lifestyle which might be altered, in however small a way, so as to accept something of the responsibility which is ours, to make some contribution (no matter how small) to the solution and to act as a witness (whether publicly visible or not) to God's kingdom. That alteration can be turned into a commitment which is written on a piece of paper and (perhaps folded) placed in a bowl or basket in front of the pinboard as an offering.

Watching with the crucified Christ

We have tried to see where our responsibilities lie, we have made an act of contrition and we have made a small penance . . . but absolution in the traditional sense is not possible. We shall continue to be involved in sins against humanity and creation whether we like it or not. In this final part of the exercise we therefore acknowledge the pain of our powerlessness in the face of our corporate responsibility.

> Yet ours were the sufferings he was bearing,
> ours the sorrows he was carrying,
> while we thought of him as someone being punished
> and struck with affliction by God;
> whereas he was being wounded for our rebellions,
> crushed because of our guilt;
> the punishment reconciling us fell on him,
> and we have been healed by his bruises. (Isa. 53.4–5 NJB)

A crucifix is hung or placed in the centre of the pinboard as the words of Isaiah are read. The group is invited to meditate upon the cross as the place where God takes responsibility for all the pain and suffering over which we have no power.

The meditation is probably best left as silent but could be concluded with suitable words which do not attempt to reduce the magnitude of what is happening but bring us back to God's overwhelming redeeming and reconciling love. One suggestion for this purpose is the poem 'Still falls the Rain' by Edith Sitwell (which can be found in *The Faber Book of Religious Verse*, ed. Helen Gardner).

True religion . . . always starts from the felt need for renewal . . . and sin is an obstruction to this new awareness. Sin is resignation to a stale and opaque world without depth or meaning.

PHILIP TOYNBEE

8
Journalling

Travelling is a brutality. It forces you to trust strangers and to lose sight of all that familiar comfort of home and friends. You are constantly off balance. Nothing is yours except the essential things – air, sleep, dreams, the sea, the sky – all things tending towards the eternal or what we imagine of it.

CESARE PAVESE

Introduction

Many people find that to 'think things through on paper' allows new ideas, insights and attitudes to develop which otherwise might only have emerged with the help of a counsellor or spiritual director. Some people maintain a regular journal, often over many years; others will keep a journal only during a retreat or at a time of stress or decision-making.

To write a journal may not seem to be an activity of prayer but 'journalling' may help people to ask the underlying question, 'Where is God in all this?' or 'Where does it seem that God may be wanting me to go in all this?' Some may find it useful to have a written dialogue with God (or with the person of Jesus if this seems easier) because this pushes us to *listen*, though we must beware lest we take our own selfish wishes to be the voice of God – it happens all too often!

Offered here is a list of four exercises:

(1) Rags to riches

Imagine that through no fault of your own you were suddenly reduced to dire poverty. What things in your possession or lifestyle would you struggle hardest to preserve? Why are these things so important to you?

Suppose again that you inherited a fabulous fortune. What would you do first? How would you use your new-found wealth?

Finally, play God. What would you change or create in our world to make it as you feel it should be?

(2) A difficult patch

Write discursively about any difficult patch which you have encountered in the past or the present. Describe your feelings as well as what happened.

Continue writing to reflect on whether and how you can perceive something of God at work in that situation either at the time or subsequently.

In the light of the writing do you think your perception of that situation has altered at all, even if in only a small way?

(3) What time is it?

Imagine a twenty-four-hour clock. What time is it on the clock at this time of your life, and why? Write about this.

    Is it too late for . . . . ?
    Is it too soon for . . . . ?
    Now is the time for . . . .

(4) Twenty-four hours

Where has God been in your life in the past twenty-four hours? In the difficult things as well as in the good things? What new insights have there been for you to gain as you think back? What was God trying to say to you which perhaps you missed at the time? Is there any action he seems to be pressing you to take? Write discursively about all these.

---

(5) 'Dear God, I hate you!'

One of the contributors to this book offered an example of how she had used this 'journalling' idea for herself. It is a piece of very powerful and moving writing which we reproduce just as we received it – as a witness to the potential value of journalling.

The tradition of Christianity to which I belonged for the best part of forty years meant that my brand of faith was a somewhat 'whiter than white', nicer than nice, and ultra-polite business.

I talked to God in prayer in the way in which my parents had taught me to relate to important people – with smiles, reticence and courtesy (lots of 'pleases' and 'thank you's'). I did my best to maintain a safe distance between God and my emotions – for I had been taught as a child: 'Nice people keep themselves to themselves . . . especially when around those who are deemed to be "the important ones".' Rarely, if ever, did God get much in the way of an honest communication from me during all those years – even when I was depressed or beside myself with fear, fury or grief. He was far too important for that.

A few years ago things began to alter for me as I began to change as a person. To my surprise, I discovered (belatedly in my life) that God could be as much a part of my inner, 'feeling' world as of my outer, rational self. I then began to realize that there were certain matters which I must sort out with God or I might burst with pent-up emotion, be spiritually crippled or find my faith evaporating.

I had a problem. How could I, in mid-life, start to express in prayer those feelings about which I had been inarticulate in the past? Habits die hard. 'You could try writing a letter to God', suggested my spiritual director tentatively, knowing that I communicate easily with pen and paper.

So I started to write a series of letters which sometimes began with the greeting, 'Dear God, I hate you!' In them I plainly, colourfully, and using more expletives than a well-brought-up lady like me is supposed to know, began to tell God just how I felt about his treatment of me. My anger spilled over the paper at (what I then perceived to be) his indifference to the tricky plight of me and mine; at the way in which he had (as I then saw it) let me down and failed to keep his part of bargains we had struck; at the injustice that my children were hurt (it seemed by God); at my inner, gnawing, chronic pain at what was happening in and around me; at my absolute powerlessness to change my situation. This was the first time I was able to face just how angry I was with God and begin to share it with him.

Those letters enabled me to bring the chaos and hurt of my inner world to God, to express my feelings in all their raw ugliness, and to discover that it was permissible (by God if not all of his followers), safe and healing for me to pray in such a way. God understood it all – and instead of withdrawing from me surrounded me with his love.

At the end of this exercise I discovered that by saying 'I hate you, God!' I was in fact confirming that often love and hate go hand in hand. What really I was meaning by those words was, 'Dear God, I love and trust you enough to bring my hiddenness, my shades and shadows to you with all their unknownness and fear . . . I'm safe enough with you to be able to do this. . . .'

The exercise of 'letter-writing prayers' enabled me later to begin to articulate these feelings in silent and articulated prayer.

A journey has two inseparable companions: conflict and new beginnings.

ANON

9
Use of the Visual

Oh, we crazy-pates! What joys our eyes give us.

VINCENT VAN GOGH

Introduction

'None so blind as those who *will* not see.' That is one kind of blindness – a perverse refusal to accept reality or to accept our need to change in response to reality as it is. Many of us will find ourselves becoming aware of that wilful kind of blindness as we try to confront the reality of God in prayer. Painful, yet salutary.

But our literal physical sight can be a helpful part of prayer. It may well be sensible to counsel small children to shut their eyes to pray, thereby making it less likely that little Johnnie will kick Peter during assembly, but it seems a strange idea of God if we can only regard the world he has created as a distraction from prayer. Far better to use our God-given sight as an *aid* to prayer. It has been pointed out elsewhere in this book that words (with which Christians are so easily obsessed) are at one remove from reality, whereas what we *see* is reality itself.

In the use of our eyes, as in so much else in prayer, we are brought up against our frequent inability to stop and stare and wonder – to *take time*. There is enough beauty in a single flower, a single piece of pottery, the shape of a tree, a single good Christmas card to provide us with enough material for a whole prayer session.

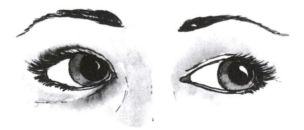

Again, some people find the use of sight – or sight-with-imagination – more helpful than others, but if we largely go through life with our eyes closed, it will enlarge our understanding of God if we sometimes try to 'pray with our eyes open'.

God looked on all that he had made and it was very good.

If *God* took the time to look at it so should we . . . and we, too, shall discover that it is very good.

---

(1) With pencil and paper

Most of us tend to say 'I cannot draw!' But all of us can scribble or draw little pin people; all of us can draw simple diagrams which show things in relation to each other. Often this kind of work with paper and pencil reveals new patterns and new insights which can be turned into prayer. It is so easy to think we can only use words in our expression of God. Probably little pin people are no more inadequate to express God in our lives than many of the very trite words we often use!

In doing this exercise it is wise to remember that your drawings are for your eyes only!

(a) Draw some representation of what God means to you. Then depict yourself in relationship to God in whatever manner seems appropriate to you.

(b) Either on another sheet of paper or by altering your first drawing now depict how you WISH God might be for you and how you WISH you could be in relationship with God.

(c) Now draw onto either sheet the things which seem to get in the way of God being for you as you would wish.

(d) Now PRAY your pictures in silence in whatever way is helpful to you. For example, ponder your pictures in the light of one of the sayings below:

I have come in order that you might have life – life in all its fullness. (John 10.10 GNB)

Whoever finds me finds life. (Prov. 8.35 REB)

Or ask God for what you feel you need: give thanks for all God has made known of himself to you.

(2) Contrasting images

(a) Choose a reasonably well-known Bible story. In this exercise the Garden of Gethsemane is the story.

(b) It may be helpful first to see what *facts* about the story of Jesus in the Garden of Gethsemane you can recall, and to write down these on a piece of paper. It is most important that you *don't* look up the story in the Bible, but use your memory; and that you just recall facts, not opinions or interpretations about the story.

(c) Now draw how you visualize the scene in the garden. If you find it quite impossible to draw, then try to describe the scene in words. The aim is to help you clarify your own visual image of the scene. This may take 10–15 minutes.

(d) Then reflect on the experience. It may be helpful at this point to read how the Bible records the scene.

Note: (i) With the Garden of Gethsemane it can be instructive at the end to compare the accounts in the synoptic Gospels, Matt. 26.36ff, Mark 14.32ff, Luke 22.39ff, with that in John 18.1ff.
(ii) It can be very interesting to visit a place like the National Gallery to see how different artists have imagined the scene; or to have a collection of slides/postcards of paintings to look at.

(e) End with a time of silence, before God.

---

(3) Meditating with pictures

This is an exercise which leads from the *meditative* approach to prayer towards the *contemplative*.

Collection and provision of pictures

These may be postcards, photographs or pictures from newspapers and magazines, preferably in colour and depicting a wide variety of subjects, not necessarily religious. It is good to build up your own collection.

Method

Look carefully at one meditation card.

The meditative part of the exercise (which may last up to 10 minutes) involves finding out what it represents, imagining what it is or guessing.

Next, relate to it, having feelings of like, dislike, curiosity, etc.

Then try to make some link with the card in a personal way. Perhaps it can be related to our prayer life. Think, ponder, muse, meditate.

After a time, stop the thinking process and simply look at the picture. Close your eyes if helpful and just be present to your picture with all that it has come to mean.

The exercise may be brought to a close in any suitable way after about a total of 20-30 minutes.

Pictures may be selected to follow themes (e.g. the Passion) or they may be a random collection of evocative pictures.

---

(4) A meditation on four meanings of the word 'spring'

(Based on the definitions and some of the ideas in Stephen Verney, *Into the New Age*, Fontana 1976, pp. 66-79)

Visual aids used

A candle; four pictures - a person leaping over a gap, a coiled spring, the countryside in springtime, and a waterfall or other flowing water.

We are going to meditate on the word 'spring', and on how its different meanings turn up in our daily lives and in our lives as Christians.

(a) A leap

When we are out walking we sometimes have to leap over a ditch or up a bank. Or, at work, we have to change jobs or patterns of work and this may involve quite a leap. We may even find change in our church worship. It is a jump from the known to the unknown, from the well-worn to the new. It may be a leap in faith, trusting in God to hold us up and to guide us. He will go with us as we take the risk and leap, and he will show us the way in the unknown places.

Silence (5 minutes)

(b) Springtime

We find we are in a fresh, green country, which is being renewed by new life bursting out everywhere. There are still some familiar landmarks, but even they look fresher. There is colour, sound and bright

94

light. The words, 'The Light of Christ' in the Easter liturgy give everything a new look and new life. But spring also shows up the dust and dirt, and we find we have to do some spring-cleaning in ourselves, so that the light can get to our darkest corners and make us wholly new.

Silence (5 minutes)

(c) A coiled spring

This kind of spring is resilient; it returns to its original shape whenever it is pulled, or contracted (as in a chair). In us, this spring might be thought of as the power of God. So we can be stretched by overwork, the cares of our daily lives, responding to an emergency, and God restores us to our original shape. Or we can be sat upon, diminished in some way, and he brings us back to the shape in which he made us, and in which he wants and loves us.

Silence (5 minutes)

(d) A spring of water

This spring bursts out of the rocks, or from the ground beneath us, and flows through the land freshening and revitalizing as it goes. Even its sound is refreshing when we are hot and dry. It provides water to drink and to wash in.

So we come to think of Jesus at the well in Samaria, and his promise to give that woman, and us, 'living water'. 'Whoever drinks the water I give him will never thirst. Indeed, the water I give him will become in him a spring of water welling up to eternal life.' (John 4.14 NIV)

Silence (5 minutes)

Close with some well-known words by Charles Wesley:

> Thou of life the Fountain art,
> Freely let me take of thee,
> Spring thou up within my heart,
> Rise to all eternity.

Other words will be equally suited to this method of reflection and meditation, for example, 'cross', 'grace', 'light', and 'green'.

95

(5) Meditating with an icon

An icon is not necessarily a picture, but can be any meaningful image.

In this exercise there are three phases:

(a) Look steadily and with concentration at the image. You may offer a prayer individually or as a group, silently or aloud.

The prayer now will be silent, with any words spoken inwardly.

(b) Close your eyes and take the image into you mind. Think about it.

(c) Let the image sink down and be lost in your heart, the centre of your being. The prayer may now be wordless and image-less.

Christ exists in all things that are.

GREGORY OF NAZIANZUS

10
Symbols

Science is the use of the mind to explore nature, while religion is the use of love to explore reality.

DAVID L. EDWARDS

_____

Introduction

A mathematical symbol has a single, clear-cut meaning. You either know the meaning of the symbol or you do not (though you might sometimes guess at it). It is unfortunate that the same word 'symbol' when used in the context of literature, art or religion, needs to be understood in a very different way. All too easily might a teacher be tempted to say, for example, that candles in church *mean* this . . ., or a procession in church *means* that . . . or incense *means* something else.

Once we have done that kind of thing we have lost the mystery and the imagination, for a non-mathematical symbol has no single, clear-cut meaning: a symbol may mean different things at different times; a symbol may suddenly have a new meaning for us so that like a person we love, we can *go on* finding something new in them. ('Behold I make all things new.')

The exercises in this chapter may help you to deepen your understanding of symbols used in the religious sense of the word. The first two use 'light' as a symbol and the third, a stone or pebble. The fourth invites you to choose an object, something familiar and not particularly special, to use in a meditation that allows that object possibly to become a symbol of something deeper, through the use of Scripture and silence. The next exercise invites you to make a mandala which you can use for understanding yourself and for prayer. The last exercise invites you to meditate using a labyrinth, an ancient symbol of 'the journey'.

By using symbols for prayer, you may be helped to an awareness of a variety of symbols pointing beyond yourself to God as you go about your daily life, and also to be more aware of your own personal symbols for which there is a prayer exercise elsewhere in this book (see chapter 4 on the use of the imagination, p. 44).

The first two exercises in this chapter both use the light of a candle to symbolize Christ. The Bible speaks of Christ as the Light of the World.

'Light' is only one of the picture words we use when we try to talk of God. No words can be adequate to describe God; the best we can do with language is to hope that each word we use may ENLIGHTEN us just a little. But the WORD 'light' is at one remove from the real thing; words are in the head, words are intellectual. What is more, words can sometimes get in the way between God and us because God is reality, not just words in the head. God needs to communicate with us in the heart, in the whole of our being, not simply in our minds.

---

(1) Light

(a) Begin with some relaxation or quietening down.

(b) Light a candle and if possible sit in a room dark enough for the candle to shed some light.

Look at the flame and observe the life that is in it – its movement and brightness, how the flame is never still. Allow yourself time to watch the light it sheds, to watch the darkness and the shadows. Light is itself the gift of God.

Give yourself some more time in which to get in touch with the light of Christ shining in the dark places of the world. There is no need to try to think interesting thoughts – just stay with the light.

'The light shines on in the darkness and the darkness has never quenched it.' (John 1.5)

The darkness will *never* overcome the light. As long as the light burns it is more powerful than all the darkness in the world.

Recall that Christ promised he would dwell in us. How easily we forget this! His light is *in* you, not simply outside you, and that light is wanting to shine out through you and enlighten the world. Give some time to this too, picturing the light in the heart of you, waiting till you allow God to make you, too, a light in a dark world.

100

(c) Think of that light shining in front of you and within you being carried out into the dark places of the world. *Think* of the dark places in the world and of the people you know who are in darkness and in need of light. Pray for them either in silence or aloud.

(d) Finally extinguish the candle but pause to recall that the light continues to burn inside you. Return to this thought whenever you can. 'He who follows me,' said Jesus, 'shall have the light of life' (John 8.12).

○ (2) The Light of Christ

This exercise with candles can be used to express the corporate nature of prayer, and the way the Spirit of Christ grows in us when we pray.

The leader will need to provide a small candle for each member of the group (baptismal or votive candles are ideal), and a large candle to be placed in the centre of the room. Don't forget the matches! A cassette player and a suitable tape will also be needed. Pachelbel's Kanon is ideal, but a Taizé chant would do equally as well.

All sit or stand in a circle round the central candle.

LEADER: Jesus said: 'I am the light of the world; anyone who follows me will not be walking in the dark, but will have the light of life.' (John 8.12)

Light the central candle.

LEADER: The light of Christ has come into the world.

Short silence.

LEADER: At the centre of each one of us is a spark given to us by God at our baptism. This spark is the spirit of prayer, God's gift to each member of the Body of Christ. The candle you have just been given represents this gift. The spark will be fanned into a flame if it is brought to Christ and allowed the space and opportunity to grow. Think of the spark within you.

Music.

LEADER: When you are ready, light your candle as a sign of the Holy Spirit within you, and return to the circle.

Pause while candles are lit.

LEADER: Remember that you never pray in isolation; the Holy Spirit always prays within you, and Jesus is always interceding for you and for all who follow him. Remember that when you pray you join thousands of people throughout the world and throughout time, many thousands of sparks fanned into many thousands of flames. Your spark can never be extinguished. The light of Christ never decreases.

If people are sitting, they should stand at this point.

LEADER: Move into groups of three. Notice how the light increases as you gather together. Pray silently for the people in your group, that their spirit of prayer may burn brightly.

Silence

LEADER: Each small group join another group. Pray silently for those who are forced to pray in hiding, in secret, in prison. (*Any other prayer may be used.*)

Silence

LEADER: Return to the circle round the central candle. Be conscious of your prayer as part of the prayer of Christians throughout earth and heaven. But remember you are not just one of a crowd. Your spirit of prayer is as individual and unique as the flame of your candle.
Let us thank God:
  – for the flame of prayer within us.
  – for all who pray throughout the world.
  – for all who have prayed through the ages.
  – for Jesus, the light of the world.

End by saying the Grace together.

○ (3) Meditation on a stone

This meditation was planned for a group at Parcevall Hall, a retreat house near the River Wharfe in Yorkshire. I have not attempted to generalize it but it could easily be made appropriate to pebbles from shingle beaches or other river deposits.

It needs at least half an hour. One hour would be better for groups that are used to silence. Pause for a few minutes at each new paragraph. In the final section (opening with an asterisk) make the pauses longer.

Materials

A pile of stones.
A large glass bowl full of water.
Cassette recorder and tape (e.g. 'Romantic Harp Music of the Nineteenth Century' played by Susan Drake).

Introductory music.

Pause for directions:

Will you each pick up a stone from the pile? Any one will do. We are going to

use them as the focus for our meditation. Will you hold your stone in your palm while you take time to relax in whatever way you are used to . . . be specially aware of your breathing.

Music

When you feel you have got out of your thinking into your feeling mode – I use these words in their normal, untechnical sense – begin to make friends with your stone.

Under God your stone has things to tell you. Try to put yourself into an attitude of attentive listening.

Experience your stone – not as an isolated pebble, but as part of creation. Engage with the time when it was an integral part of one of those great blocks which built the homes and halls of the West Riding.

It is a little brother of those blocks, but infinitely more experienced.

Enter imaginatively into its journey. Feel the splitting, and the pounding; the ice and the great floods; the churning and the polishing; and the little ripples which also played their part in fashioning it.

And to what end? Discuss with your stone its possible future. Will it turn the ankle of a walker, and cause an accident?
– Or be thrown at a window by a violent teenager?
– Or cobble a path?

– Or be decorated and given as a present?
– Or help someone's prayer?
– Or might it stay stuck in an eddy for ever?

Now explore your stone for its own sake. It is unique. Feel it. Taste it. Smell it.

Are there rough places? sharp angles? unexpected smoothnesses? interesting markings? bits of quartzite? colours? beautiful lines? uglinesses?

*Now, in a longer silence, let the stone you have come to know so well, speak to you about yourself:

– about your own journey up to now.

– about where you came from, and where you are going.

– about your own sharp corners and rough surfaces.

– about your own beauty and colour.

– and about your own potential for the future. . . . What are the options? What will you be doing with what you have?

When you are ready, become aware

of your surroundings, and of your companions.

Bring your stone, and plunge it with the rest into the water. Stay with it long enough to rejoice in the trans-formation and life water brings, even to the most beautiful stone.

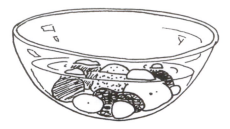

Then return to your seat, and spend some time blessing the Lord for your baptism, and relishing the com-panionship of your fellow pilgrims.

○ (4) Choose your own object

The aim is to allow individuals to pray through symbols in Scripture, making the most of the sense of touch and the ability to use symbolism and association.

Place a range of objects in the centre of the room before the group members arrive. Make sure there are more objects than the number of people expected.

As people arrive the objects will act as an 'icebreaker' causing comments and speculation.

When the group is assembled ask them to each select an object that suits them.

Invite them to handle the object and then, in silence, use it to centre themselves.

The leader then reads prepared short passages of Scripture which relate to the objects chosen by the group members, pausing for a few moments between each one.

A concordance is a helpful way to select suitable passages which should be short. If they are taken from an event the reading should be long enough for the hearer to identify the event, but should not describe it exhaustively.

The main communication in prayer for the participant is through the object. The words may suggest the prayer but must not take over from the object.

The range of objects and of verses should, hopefully, be wide enough to embrace, as far as possible, the character and the situation of all the participants.

The main period of time should be spent in silence, allowing the participants to pray through their objects.

Suggested passages for some objects:

Basket: Mark 8.19 (JB)

'When I broke the five loaves among the five thousand, how many baskets full of scraps did you collect?' They answered 'Twelve'.

Bread: Matt. 6.10–11 (JB)

Our Father in heaven,
may your name be held holy,
your kingdom come,
your will be done,
on earth as in heaven.
Give us today our daily bread.

Candle: Matt. 5.14–16 (JB)

You are the light of the world. A city built on a hill-top cannot be hidden. No one lights a lamp to put it under a tub; they put it on the lampstand where it shines for everyone in the house. In the same way your light must shine in the sight of men, so that, seeing your good works, they may give the praise to your Father in heaven.

Coin: Matt. 6.24 (JB)

No one can be the slave of two masters; he will either hate the first and love the second, or treat the first with respect and the second with scorn. You cannot be the slave both of God and of money.

Earthen vessel: 2 Cor. 4.7 (JB)

We are only the earthenware jars that hold this treasure, to make it clear that such an overwhelming power comes from God and not from us.

Footwear: Matt. 10.8–10 (JB)

Cure the sick, raise the dead, cleanse the lepers, cast out devils. You received without charge, give without charge. Provide yourselves with no gold or silver, not even with a few coppers for your purses, with no haversack for the journey or spare tunic or footwear or a staff, for the workman deserves his keep.

Fruit: Matt. 7.15–20 (JB)

Beware of false prophets who come to you disguised as sheep but underneath are ravenous wolves. You will be able to tell them by their fruits. Can people pick grapes from thorns, or figs from thistles? In the same way, a sound tree produces good fruit but a rotten tree bad fruit. A sound tree cannot bear bad fruit, nor a rotten tree bear good fruit. Any tree that does not produce good fruit is cut down and thrown on the fire. I repeat, you will be able to tell them by their fruits.

Keys: Matt. 16.18–19 (JB)

'So I now say to you: You are Peter and on this rock I will build my church. And the gates of the underworld can never hold out against it. I will give you the keys of the kingdom of heaven; whatever you bind on earth will be considered bound in heaven; whatever you loose on earth will be considered loosed in heaven.' Then he gave the disciples strict orders not to tell anyone that he was the Christ.

Pillow or cushion: Mark 4.38–9 (JB)

Then it began to blow a gale and the waves were breaking into the boat so that it was almost swamped. But Jesus was in the stern, his head on the cushion, asleep. They woke him and said to him, 'Master, do you not care? We are going down!' And he woke up and rebuked the wind and said to the sea, 'Quiet now! Be calm!' And the wind dropped, and all was calm again.

Salt: Matt. 5.13 (JB)

You are the salt of the earth. But if salt becomes tasteless, what can make it salty again? It is good for nothing, and can only be thrown out to be trampled underfoot by men.

Stone: John 8.7 (JB)

As they persisted with their question, he looked up and said, 'If there is one of you who has not sinned, let him be the first to throw a stone at her.'

(5) The mandala

The mandala is a symbol of the whole self, by which self-knowledge may grow, and hence knowledge of God.

All you need is a sheet of A4 paper, a plate to draw round (or a compass) which will fit entirely on the paper, a pencil and rubber, and some coloured pens with various sizes of point – some very fine, some medium and some thick along with some highlighters for fainter background colour.

Cut down the paper to make a square.
Put the plate in the middle of the square and draw round it faintly in pencil.
Now you are ready to begin!

The circle stands for your self, your whole self, conscious and unconscious.
You now draw and colour the circle as you feel led.
What goes at the centre is likely to have special importance, as for most of us that will be saying something about what is at the heart of us.

Sometimes an idea for the mandala will have come to us some time before, but usually it comes as we look at the empty circle. Some sort of loose geometrical design is often the starting point. It might be the kind of pattern suggested by the different parts of a flower, such as a rose, as you look on it. Or a spiral starting at the centre of the circle. Or one can begin from the centre with a motif or pattern that seems to belong there. An overall pattern may emerge from this. There will be scope for using different colours for different areas thus marked out.

Once some kind of pattern is taking shape, other less regular features may suggest themselves. The spiral may develop the features of a curled-up shell for instance, or snakes may appear threatening or embracing the centre; lions, horses, doorways, gallows, trees have sometimes emerged.

In the colouring of the background areas it may be that dark and shadowy areas appeared. These may be suggestive of the shadow areas of personality. Snakes and sharks may appear in them, or they may be soil in which trees are rooted. There may be other areas expressive of light and beauty, perhaps revealing themselves through yellow or gold colouring.

The perimeter began as a pencilled circle. This may develop into a border, perhaps curving in and out of the original circle. There might be a border zone within the circle. The border or zone may be broken through by lines or wider breaks. It may feel right to extend the mandala right to the edge of the square, so that the circle, as such, almost disappears.

It should be said that no special skills in drawing or design are required for this exercise. It is for yourself and it has to look right only to you. Continue colouring and putting in features until you are satisfied with the result.

So what does it mean? Like a dream, it can only be properly interpreted by the one who made it. We are likely to find that the meaning grows over time as we return to reflect on it at later intervals, particularly if we keep our mandalas and a dated sequence results.

Colours are significant: gold, perhaps, for the goal of the journey which already lures us; dark greys or browns for the shadow which both threatens and resources life; green for human feelings and natural growth; blue for the sea of the unconscious.

The centre is of course our centre. The border may be to do with the outside world – a solid unbroken line or heavy border pattern suggesting isolation, while at other times there is no very clear marking of the perimeter. Or there may be a violent breach suggesting some powerful happening or influence is erupting from outside.

An overall spiral pattern can suggest a rotating movement, like a catherine wheel. This may be gentle or rapid, even tumultuous as though spun by a powerful wind. Jung suggests that clockwise spirals express the unconscious coming into consciousness, while anti-clockwise ones suggest the opposite, a rather sinister and regressive state of mind. He suggests too that animals represent different kinds of unconscious psychic states, perhaps strong feelings or influences of anger, envy, jealousy or love, below the surface of the conscious mind. But other people's interpretations can only be suggestions and

hints for us to be able to find our own.

Some (with the proviso of the last paragraph in mind) will find it useful to draw mandalas in a group with others and to discuss them afterwards. For others it will be a more solitary exercise. Its interest and value are greatly increased the more we do it and the more we have a past history to look through. Patterns and symbols appear, develop and disappear, and interpretations change. But it may be a mistake to draw too many mandalas – inspiration deadens and the sense of something sent dies away. It may be right to draw several in the space of days and then not another for a year or more.

According to Jung and others, in Eastern practice mandalas may take on something of the shape of a ground-plan of a monastic enclosure, often circular within a square; and such mandalas are particularly related to the spiritual life as such. Or we may find they relate more widely to our lives as a whole.

Further reading: C. G. Jung, *Collected Works*, vol. 9: *The Archetypes and the Collective Unconscious* (Routledge 1978); see in particular 'Concerning Mandala Symbolism' (with a footnote giving other references in Jung's collected works).

(6) The labyrinth *(see over)*

Eastern contemplative traditions use symbols such as the mantra and mandala as a means of centring the mind. Psychologists like Jung have seen great significance in such symbols. Television programmes have revealed to those of us who live in the West how the act of painting a prayer wheel, or portraying it in stones or coloured rice, is in itself a process of profound meaning.

The mandala is not unknown in Christian tradition, an obvious example being the rose windows of the great cathedrals. More prevalent in Western Christianity, however, is the primitive labyrinth design, which with its twisting and tortuous path was adopted in medieval times to symbolize the pilgrimage to the Holy Land, or the way to salvation through the cycles of life, death and resurrection.

Recent years have seen a revival in the art of making garden labyrinths and mazes (the former being distinguished by having only one path) but an ephemeral indoor one can be made at far less expense and trouble. The process is a contemplative activity in its own right: a dedicated act of attention and true prayer.

The labyrinth depicted embraces the two main characteristics of medieval Christian designs: an equal-armed cross and rotational symmetry. Its construction, using three rolls of white soft toilet tissue on a cord carpet base, took just over an hour, and it was used as the centre-piece for a contemplative prayer session at 'Wychcroft', a diocesan conference centre, during a summer school of the Southwark Ordination Course.

Starting at the centre, the only technical skill to be mastered is the necessary double fold at each corner. Windows should be closed against draughts and doors locked against clumsy two-legged or four-legged intruders! The finished result has a strange, fragile beauty.

Alternatively you might like to construct your own labyrinth using soft boards, pins and strong cotton. Each person would need to have a copy of the design. Work on the labyrinth for a set time in silence, then have a time of meditation.

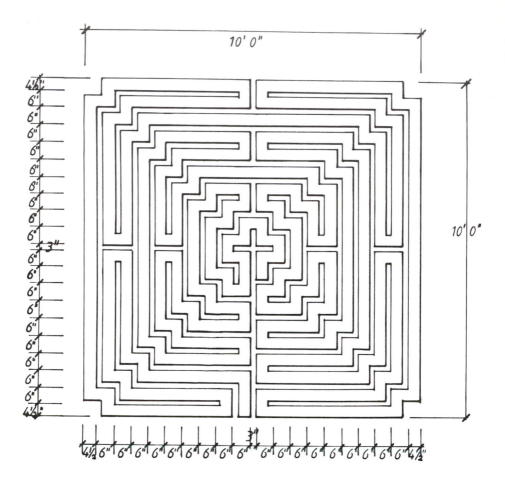

We are put on earth for a little space that we may learn to bear the beams of love.

WILLIAM BLAKE

110

11
Prayer and the Body

Do not disdain your body, for the soul is just as safe in its body as in the Kingdom of Heaven.

MECHTILDE OF MAGDEBURG

Introduction

If there is one theme that runs through every section of this book it is that prayer is a much wider phenomenon than we have often thought. Or, to put it another way, we all pray a great deal more than we may have realized. This is a great help in removing the heavy weight of guilt that many people feel when they think that they 'do not pray enough'.

The exercises which follow are an attempt to acknowledge the often-forgotten fact that we can pray with our bodies as well as with our minds. All too often Christians (and others) have come dangerously near to the heresy which says that the spirit is good, while the body is somehow, if not evil, 'not quite nice', or a distraction from God.

But the Old Testament is very clear that humankind is a totality of body, mind and spirit: mind and spirit need a body through which to express themselves. The trouble only comes in when body and spirit are pulling each other apart in different directions; in a truly integrated Christian, body, mind and spirit pull together in the same direction – towards God in love and worship and service.

Jesus himself used the body – how frequently he touched people to heal them, how frequently he uses homely illustrations of things perceived by the senses, just as the Old Testament prophets use physical symbols – a potter and his clay, a basket of figs.

That which is unloved tends to turn nasty: that is a simple fact about the world God has created, and if our bodies are neglected and unloved they, too, will turn nasty. Much better to use our bodies as a part of our prayer. If you cannot see these exercises as prayer in themselves, perhaps you can see them as ways into prayer.

○ **(1) Touch, scent and taste**

Introduce to the group a palette of textures, smells and tastes. Perhaps the following might be considered:

> Ice in a glass bowl with stainless steel tweezers;
> A plant in a clay pot;
> A collection of different stones in a bowl;
> A breadboard, bread and knife.

Sections (a) and (b) may be used independently or together.

(a) Pass each of the objects around. Smell, taste, touch as appropriate. It might help to increase your sensitivity to touch if after seeing the object you then close your eyes. Say to yourself as you handle each of the items, 'The earth is the Lord's and all its fullness', or some other statement about the created order.

Think of each item as good in itself, though morally neutral. Then think of each material and how people can use it for a good or an evil purpose. For example, in the case of the bread, breadboard and knife, think of the knife either cutting bread or doing damage to another human being; think of the West with food mountains while others starve; think of the wood used for providing shelter or as an instrument of torture, etc. Don't worry if you can't think of a good and bad use for everything.

Pray for people who suffer from abuse of what you are touching. Pray for the proper use of God's creation.

(b) Take one of the stones out of the bowl and pass it round the group. Allow each member of the group to hold the stone for perhaps two minutes and ask all the others to pray for that person silently as he or she holds the stone. The person holding the stone may ask the group for prayer in a particular area or for a particular thing that concerns them.

After two minutes the stone is passed on to the next person in the circle. The signal to pass on may be given by the use of a short prayer or chorus said or sung communally. For example:

Jesus, take me as I am,
I can come no other way.
Take me deeper into You,
Make my flesh life melt away.
Make me like a precious stone,
Crystal clear and finely honed.
Life of Jesus shining through,
Giving glory back to You.

Visit . . . . [*name of person*] we pray you, Lord;
drive far from her/him all the snares of the enemy;
may your holy angels dwell with her/him and guard her/him in peace;
and may your blessing be always upon her/him;
through Jesus Christ our Lord. Amen.

Lord, you are in our midst, we are called by your name. Do not desert us, O Lord our God. (Jer. 14.9 REB)

(no. 127, *Mission Praise*; D. Bryant © 'Thank You Music' 1978)

---

(2) A sense of touch

If our bodies as well as our heads and our hearts can provide a path to God or a window into God then *all* our senses can play their part.

The sense many people are afraid to use in their faith is the sense of touch. There is a widespread fear that somehow touch equals sex. Yet there are many occasions (probably most) when there is no sexual connotation at all – a warm handshake, an arm round someone in distress, or even those bear-hugs after scoring a goal on the football field.

The following prayer exercises are gentle enough not to frighten anyone! They could either form two prayer exercises or a single extended exercise. They start from an awareness of our own bodies, continue with feeling an object, and then use the sense of touch in prayer for healing, rounding off with holding hands in a circle to emphasize our oneness in Christ.

(a) Loosen any tight clothing and remove your shoes. Then centre down by becoming aware of your body, starting from the toes, working upwards, paying particular attention to areas of tension or discomfort. Give thanks for the marvellous complexity of the human body, which despite our ill-treatment of it usually serves us so well. Allow about 5 minutes for this.

Take and hold a medium-sized stone or pebble and feel its weight, its shape, its cracks and bumps. Ponder the millions of years your stone has

115

been in existence, the earth when it began, the stone's history, what has gone on around it in the natural world, in the human world. That stone matters to God as a part of his creation; his world would not be complete without it, just as God's creation would not be complete without YOU. He needs you, too. How do you feel about your stone now? (Allow about 10 minutes for this section.)

Put your stone down. How do you feel about relinquishing it? Reluctant? Have you come to love that stone and its history just a little bit? If we have come to cherish our little stone in so short a time and do not want to lose it, how much more must WE matter to GOD! Short silence. (cf Jonah 4.10–11)

(b) A sense of touch is a way of literally getting 'in touch' with our feelings and with God. Jesus frequently used the sense of touch. Read aloud Luke 6.53–6 and think about it for a few minutes. Why did Jesus often touch people when he healed them?

None of us is a whole person; all of us have undeveloped potentialities, or gifts we have wasted. Most of us have anxieties or some kind of neurosis. Many have physical illnesses. We are now going to lay hands on each other to ask God, through the use of touch, for wholeness. Go round the circle in turn with the person on either side of each laying hands on the person between them. Before the laying on of hands

some group members may like to tell the group what aspect of wholeness they are particularly asking for; others may prefer this to be between themselves and God.

This may be done either in silence or a leader may say some short prayer over each person, e.g.

N., may the Lord in his love and mercy uphold you by the grace and power of the Holy Spirit.

or

We lay our hands on you in the name of our Lord Jesus Christ. May he give you that healing and wholeness he wills for you and those you pray for. May his strength and peace fill you now and always.

or

God of grace, power and mercy; look on your servant N. with love. Give her/him courage and confidence in your protection, and lead her/him to peace, through Jesus Christ our Lord.

At the end of this time, members may like to ask the whole group to pray for others in need of healing or wholeness.

A leader may then say some such prayer as:

Almighty God, Father of all mercies, we thank you for all your gifts of healing and forgiveness, for the grace to love and care for each other, for your hidden blessings and for all you have in store for us, for everything, whether joy or sorrow, whereby you are drawing us to yourself through Jesus Christ our Lord.

End the session by standing, holding hands in a circle and saying the Grace together. Do not hurry to release hands, but ponder for a few moments the truth that 'we are the Body of Christ' and that in him we are 'all one body'.

Movement in prayer

Movement in prayer may be new to some; so may spontaneous creation of prayer. But be bold and try one of these exercises:

(3) Walking

Many people find that to take a walk will encourage them to pray as they walk but attention to the actual process of walking can be a prayer in itself.

We seldom give attention to this process, and yet it involves the whole of the body. To ponder the activity of walking can lead to a sense of wonder at the complexity and (usually!) efficiency of the body God has given us.

In a large room or hall, or in a garden, walk VERY slowly indeed around the outside of the room or garden, being aware of very deliberately lifting the leg . . . moving the leg forward . . . placing the heel, then the toe, on the ground . . . being aware of the shift of weight in the whole body . . . and so on.

After a while pause and read aloud Psalm 139.12–16:

For you have created my inward parts;
you knit me together in my mother's womb;
I will praise you for you are to be feared;
fearful are your acts and wonderful your works.

You knew my soul and my bones were not hidden from you;
when I was formed in secret and woven in the depths of the earth

Your eyes saw my limbs when they were yet imperfect; and in your book were all my members written;

Day by day they were fashioned; and not one was late in growing.

Ponder this for a little while. A theme may now be introduced, and you may choose to walk as slowly as your sense of balance will allow (still very slowly indeed, but at your own pace), while pondering a given theme, e.g.

I am on my journey to God . . .
I am one of the shepherds travel-

ling to Bethlehem . . .
I am one of the wise men following the star . . .
I am accompanying Jesus as he goes into the desert for his forty days in the wilderness – or as he leaves the desert to begin his ministry . . .

○ (4) Walking encounters

This will require space enough to walk round a room.

Ask people to move at different speeds – fast, slow.
Ask them to become aware of the people in the room with them.
Direct them periodically to pause and look at the person nearest them and then move on.

Music might be played quietly in the background.

Then invite people to find a phrase, a word . . . or look at each other and ponder or talk about a concern . . .
For example, at a meeting concerned with social responsibility the leader invited people at the pauses to share briefly their concern about homelessness, justice, single parents, poverty, etc.

End with a short period of silence and some discussion about the experience.

○ (5) The wheel

The next suggestion, the wheel, could be used at the start of a new prayer group or a one-off prayer session, to help people get to know each other before getting down to more formal praying. The movement encourages people truly to encounter each different person.

Preparation

The leader draws up a list of questions – about seven.

Start with simply asking each person their name or some fairly flippant kind of question.

(Let us assume that prayer is the topic for the group meeting.) The next question may be to ask for a place in the Bible where Jesus or some other person is at prayer.

This could then lead to asking about group members' own understanding of prayer.

Draw up five to seven questions.

Method

Direct everyone to stand in two circles facing one another.

The leader asks the first question. Allow a minute each way for the twosomes to give each other an answer. They should preface their answer each time with their name. Be firm on timing so that each person has a chance to answer.

Then direct everyone to move one pace to the right so that they now have a different partner facing them.

Ask the second question, and so on.

Allow time for sharing the experience at the end.

---

(6) Listening

Most of us live in a world full of noise and so can find silence quite difficult. More specifically, most of us have got so much to say, and so little opportunity to share it with somebody else who'll listen to us, that we grab every opportunity with both hands, forgetting that the other person may themselves need us not to speak but rather to listen to them. So, some exercises to help us to listen:

(a) Settle down and be still. Then play a piece of quiet music (guitar music is ideal) and simply listen to it. It is important that the music is quiet, so that you have to listen hard. (10 minutes)

(b) Be still and be aware of all the sounds around you. Identify and name the sounds that you can hear, beginning with those furthest away and ending with the sounds of your own body - your breathing, heartbeat, etc. (10 minutes)

Then listen to those sounds again, and first give thanks to God for each of them in turn and secondly reflect on what God may be saying through the sounds you can hear. (10 minutes)

---

(7) Sitting at God's feet

There are two phases:

(a) Sit on your heels with the soles of your feet turned up; with back, neck and head straight; hands resting on knees. (This can be uncomfortable or even impossible for some people; in which case, you can either use a prayer stool, kneel upright or sit cross-legged.) This can be a very good, prayerful posture.

(b) Turn the head to the right, then to the left, then up and finally down. You can pray for other people, on your 'right' and your 'left' (West/East, sheep/goats, political right/left); then look 'up' to God in worship and adoration, maybe saying the Gloria (Glory be to the Father and to the Son and to the Holy Spirit. As it was in the beginning, is now and ever shall be, world without end. Amen). Then look down into your heart, as the Orthodox teach, perhaps by saying the Jesus Prayer (Lord Jesus Christ, have mercy upon me a sinner).

(8) Let my prayer rise before you like incense

Introduction

Throughout the Bible incense is often a symbol of prayer rising to God. The following exercise is designed using incense as the central focus for prayer rising to God. If you are able to use an incense burner so much the better. On the other hand you could use a fondue bowl with some 'pot-pourri'. Check that there is no smoke alarm that might be activated by the use of incense! Since the aid for our intercession is intended to be the incense it would be helpful if the room was dark so that only the smoke of the incense

can be seen. If you meet for prayer in the setting of a splendid church, which has a sense of the otherness of God, then so much the better. Furthermore, if you find yourself in such a setting you might face East – something not often done today. It is important to realize that despite the majesty of God and the immensity of the prayer ascending, God listens to each of us individually in our tiniest requests. Perhaps this approach to intercession may help us to avoid trivializing prayer and force us to question whether what we are really asking for is in his will.

The following exercise is divided into three sections of fifteen minutes each.

You may like to have some majestic music quietly in the background during the exercise provided it is used with great sensitivity. Music recorded from the Orthodox liturgy might be appropriate.

Focus on the majesty of God

Reading: Rev. 8.3–4 (JB)

Another angel, who had a golden censer, came and stood at the altar. A large quantity of incense was given to him to offer with all the prayers of the saints on the golden altar that stood in front of the throne; and so from the angel's hand the smoke of the incense went up in the presence of God and with it the prayers of all the saints.

First imagine yourself in the intimate presence of God in all his splendour – you might reflect on some of the imagery used in the Book of Revelation recalling the majesty of God and the dazzling light (Rev. 4); God surrounded by twenty-four elders with golden bowls full of incense made of the prayers of the saints (Rev. 5.8).

Allow plenty of time for this and after a period of silence and/or music say the song of the four animals:

Holy, Holy, Holy is the Lord God, the almighty: he was, he is and he is to come.

Focus on the immensity of prayers rising before God

Reading: Malachi 1.11 JB

From farthest east to farthest west my name is honoured among the nations and everywhere a sacrifice of incense is offered to my name, and a pure offering too, since my name is honoured among the nations, says the Lord Sabbaoth.

Now imagine throughout the earth the intercessions rising up to the throne of God. In your mind hear the groaning of millions of people – the groans of the living and the groans of the departed (Rev. 6.9–11) – ten thousand times ten thousand of them and thousands upon thousands (Rev. 5.11). Sense the

121

immensity of prayer before God's throne by the communion of saints.

Silence and/or background music.

> Holy, Holy, Holy is the Lord God, the almighty: he was, he is and he is to come.

Now offer your intercessions

Reading: Psalm 141.2 JB

> My prayers rise like incense
> My hands like the evening offering.

As you name before God your particular concern you might like to place a few grains of incense on the burner or light a candle and place it beside the burner and repeat the phrase from Psalm 141.2:

> My prayers rise like incense
> My hands like the evening offering.

Silence and/or background music

End by saying the Canticle from Revelation 15.3–4:

> Great and wonderful are your deeds, Lord God the Almighty: just and true are your ways, O King of the nations.

> Who shall not revere and praise your name, O Lord?
> for you alone are holy.

> All nations shall come and worship in your presence:
> for your just dealings have been revealed.

> To him who sits on the throne and to the Lamb:
> be praise and honour, glory and might for ever and ever. Amen.
> (Alternative Service Book 1980)

Prayer through music

Music plays a part in most people's lives and can be listened to on various levels of our intellect and emotions. The successful BBC radio programme 'Desert Island Discs' shows how important music is in the lives of even the most 'unmusical' of people. Music can also be used in our prayer life in various ways.

For some, music can be used as an introduction to their prayer time and maybe to round it off. For others, music *is* prayer, an excellent example being Taizé music with its repeated phrases.

It is good to be open to using a variety of styles and to be prepared to use 'secular' and even popular styles, including the use of synthesizers, as well as specifically 'religious' music.

If there are any words, having them typed out is important in that it enables you to *pray* the words as they are sung.

Different types of music can be used for different topics in the prayer session, e.g. thanksgiving, penitence, petition, intercession. A list of suggestions is given below.

It is vitally important to have good equipment for reproducing the music. It doesn't need to be expensive, but it does need to be reliable!

Care needs to be taken not to saturate the session with too much music, which if overdone could produce emotional and mental indigestion. Probably better to have too little rather than too much. If possible, put all the musical items in playing order onto a single tape with a short gap between each one. A 'pause' button is most useful.

Below are examples of music for different types of prayer. They are inevitably subjective and you will no doubt have your own ideas.

Music to introduce the session

Air on G String from J. S. Bach's Suite no. 3 in D Major
Slow movement from Serenade in E minor for Strings, Edward Elgar
Motet: Ave Verum Corpus, Byrd
Motet: Ave Verum Corpus, K 618, Mozart (EMI EL749672-4 cassette)
Concerto in D minor for two violins and orchestra, J. S. Bach
Slow movement from Symphony No. 5 in C minor, Beethoven
7th movement from Variations on a theme of Haydn, Brahms
2nd movement from Violin Concerto No. 1 in G minor, Max Bruch
Siegfried Idyll, Wagner
1st movement from Holberg Suite, opus 40, Grieg
Overture (Minuet) from 'Berenice', Handel
'Meditation' Intermezzo from 'Thaïs', Act II, Massenet
2nd movement from Violin Concerto in E minor, Mendelssohn
Symphony No. 5 in B flat major, Schubert
Träumerei 'Reverie' from Scenes of Childhood, opus 15, Schubert
Serenade in C major for Strings, Tchaikovsky

Music for thanksgiving

Anthem: For the beauty of the earth, John Rutter (Collegium)
Anthem: All things bright and beautiful, John Rutter (COL100C cassette)
Symphony No. 6, 'Pastoral', Beethoven
How lovely are thy dwellings (from *A German Requiem*), Brahms

Penitence

Adagio for strings, Samuel Barber
Jesus, remember me, 'Laudate', from *Music of Taizé*
Anthem: Lord for thy tender mercies' sake, Farrant (Collegium COL 107C)
3rd movement from Cello Concerto in E minor, Elgar
Anthem: Salvator Mundi, John Blow (EMI EL 747772-4 cassette)
Anthem: Remember not, Lord, our offences, Purcell (Conifer MCFC 152 cassette)
Anthem: Wash me thoroughly – S. S. Wesley (Meridian E770 88 record)

Approaches to Prayer

Petition

Anthem: God be in my head, John Rutter ('Gloria' Collegium COL 100 C)
Anthem: Jesu, grant me this, I pray, Edward Bairstow
Imagine, John Lennon
Anthem: Thou wilt keep him in perfect peace – S. S. Wesley

Holy Spirit

Veni Sanctus Spiritus, 'Canons and Litanies', *Music of Taizé*
Anthem: If ye love me, Tallis

Praise

Surrexit Christus, 'Resurrexit', *Music of Taizé*
Anthem: O clap your hands, Orlando Gibbons
Anthem: Exultate Deo, Palestrina
Anthem: This joyful Eastertide, arr. Charles Wood

(9) Prayer through music 1

Play a piece of music that will help you to become still. (3–5 minutes)

Silence (5 minutes)

Then play a piece of music that expresses the glory and wonder of creation or of God. (3–5 minutes)

Silence (10 minutes)

Play a piece of music that expresses joy, adoration or thanksgiving. (3–5 minutes)

Silence (10 minutes)

End by saying a short prayer and/or by saying the Grace: The grace of our Lord Jesus Christ and the love of God and the fellowship of the Holy Spirit be with us all now and for ever.

Amen.

(10) Prayer through music 2

Music can also be used to express what we hear, whether poetry or prose. After hearing a reading if we then listen to a piece of appropriate music we may find that it helps us to open up to the deeper meaning of what we have heard and by so doing to enter those deeper places within ourselves where we may encounter the living God.

Theme: Joy and Praise

Reflection: Lord, we bless you for our creation.

Music: 1st movement from Symphony No. 6, Beethoven (5–10 minutes).

Short silence (2–3 minutes).

Reading:

         . . . Magnificent
The morning rose, in memorable pomp,
Glorious as e'er I had beheld – in front,
The sea lay laughing at a distance; near,
The solid mountains shone, bright as the clouds,
Grain-tinctured, drenched in empyrean light;
And in the meadows and the lower grounds
Was all the sweetness of a common dawn –
Dews, vapours, and the melody of birds,
And labourers going forth to till the fields.
(William Wordsworth, quoted in *From Darkness to Light*, ed. Victor Gollancz, Gollancz 1956)

Music: For the beauty of the earth, John Rutter (3 minutes).

Short silence (2–3 minutes).

Joy and Praise in the use of our talents

Reading:

He was born blind with the snow on a winter's day;
The moon blank as marble stared at him from the full,
But his mother wept to see the vacant rolling of his eyes;
His father dared not look and despairingly turned away
When hands like feelers fumbled in space to pull
Fingers and lips to upturned face to recognize.
Growing older he sat in the dark learning voices by heart,
Carried on conversations with birds singing in summer trees,
Heard brooks changing their sound at floodtime, the angled dart
Of dazzled bats diving through twilight air.
But music played by wandering band or organ at the fair
Moved him to tears and fingers to invisible keys,
So that at twenty-five he began to drown the village church
With ceaseless tides of Handel, Bach and Mendelssohn,
And magnified the Lord for seven-and-thirty years,

With egg-shaped head he sat upright upon his perch,
Praying on flute we might depart in peace
Triumphant came from Egypt on the bombardon,
Made thunderstorms at will, stars race like charioteers,
Captivity to turn, the harvest to increase;
He brought sweet healing to the troubled mind,
Fearlessly opened the eyes of the blind.
('Charles' by Leonard Clark, quoted in *From Darkness to Light*)

Music: 'How lovely are thy dwellings' from *A German Requiem* (Brahms). (5 minutes)

Short silence (2–3 minutes)

Reading:

Magnificent weather. The morning seems bathed in happy peace, and a heavenly fragrance rises from mountain and shore; it is as though a benediction were laid upon us. . . . One might believe oneself in a church – a vast temple in which every being and every natural beauty has its place. I dare not breathe for fear of putting the dream to flight – a dream traversed by angels. . . .

In these heavenly moments the cry of Pauline rises to one's lips. 'I feel! I believe! I see!' All the miseries, the cares, the vexations of life, are forgotten; the universal joy absorbs us; we enter into the divine order, and into the blessedness of the Lord. Labour and tears, sin, pain, and death have passed away. To exist is to bless; life is happiness. In this sublime pause of things all dissonances have disappeared. It is as though creation were but one vast symphony, glorifying the God of goodness with an inexhaustible wealth of praise and harmony. We question no longer whether it is so or not. We have ourselves become notes in the great concert; and the soul breaks the silence of ecstasy only to vibrate in unison with the eternal joy.

(Henri-Frédéric Amiel 1821–81, quoted in *From Darkness to Light*)

Music: Finale from Symphony No. 6, Beethoven (5–10 minutes)

God, far from being put off by our sensuality, is in our sensuality.
DAME JULIAN OF NORWICH

12
Intercession

Who is a holy person? The one who is aware of others' suffering.

KABIR

Introduction

The expression 'Let us pray' is invariably taken to mean 'Let us intercede', after which the process is usually to name before God situations and people in rapid succession with the whole compass of life and concerns being embraced. Sometimes such intercessions are of just a one-word kind, 'Let us pray for the people of India', after which you are left to your own devices.

Either method can be useful, though the more words one uses the greater the danger of putting one's own interpretation on events. All of us have found that we have disagreed with the prayer offered, sometimes to the point of wanting to make our disapproval felt by leaving. Intercession has the ability to expose our prejudices in a way that few other forms of prayer do, but it does three positive things:

– it reflects the concerns and knowledge of the intercessor;
– it enables those hearing the petition to identify with those concerns and people;
– it helps the hearers to focus on where God may be calling them to be his co-workers.

What are we doing when we intercede?

The first assumption that we make in intercession is that we creatures have a personal relationship with God, who desires to respond through his love and mercy for his creatures whom he elevates to the position of co-workers for the kingdom. For Jesus' intercession was an intimate relationship with God in which he approached him not so much as a Judge, but as 'Abba', which we usually translate by the word 'Father', but perhaps might more accurately be rendered as 'Daddy'.

The normal form of address in a Christian's prayer (at least in the West) is an address to the Father, requested through the Son in the power of the Holy Spirit. Intercession therefore from beginning to end is the act of God and if we fail to see that, then we are in trouble. St Paul puts it in words like this: it is the God within us crying to God beyond us Abba, Father. Perhaps reflecting on prayer being seen in this way might make us more wary of verbose self-opinionated prayer which can often be less than helpful. There could be a danger of this particularly in the first exercise offered below.

Further, if we pray through Jesus Christ, the one who continually intercedes on our behalf, then we should be aware that we are attempting to intercede in the will and the character of Christ. We are also praying in company with all the saints (both living and departed). This should help us avoid seeing prayer as either magic or a selfish exercise, but rather as an offering of ourselves to the will of God and an asking for things that are in his will (Matt. 7.7ff) – for justice, for delivery from evil, etc. in our world. Nothing is too big to pray for (see below, Prayer for Global Issues), nothing is too small provided it is not trivial. There is, however, something offensive in interceding for something if we then believe that is all that is required. Leaving it to God and forgetting about it, when we could actually do something about it, means that our prayer has become cheap and about as effective as that of the Pharisees (Matt. 23.3). The Epistle of James has something to say about that too (Jas. 2.15–16). The Robinsonian prayer (see exercise 4) particularly helps us to avoid this trap.

If our relationship with God is essentially that of childlike trust, then there is nothing that falls beyond his concern for us his children, though we need to come to terms with why intercession offered is not answered. Jesus had to come to terms with this himself in Gethsemane (Mark 14.35 ff).

○ (1) Listening to God on behalf of one another

Here is a simple structure for a group involving listening to God on behalf of one another, contributing insights, and praying for others. The time needed depends on the size of the group, but 45 minutes should be sufficient.

(a) Invite each person in turn to share a situation they are currently praying for or a person they are concerned about. Other members of the group should simply listen without discussing or asking questions.

(b) Then, in silence, all wait on God concerning the situation or person mentioned and listen to him.

(c) If anyone is given a word, insight, Bible verse, picture, speak it out as simply as possible, without discussion. If nothing is given, stay in silence.

(d) One person should then pray, holding the situation or person briefly before God.

(e) After this concluding prayer, move on to the next person and continue as before.

(f) At the end spend a few minutes reflecting on what happened.

130

Group leader's notes

These might be described as ground rules for running the session.

(i) Tell people there should be no discussion during group time. People's contributions should be accepted at face value. (Some people find this very hard.)

(ii) Encourage people to wait in silence and listen without dashing in with words.

(iii) Encourage people to speak out if something comes to them, even if it seems rather strange. But if nothing comes, stay in silence. It must be made clear to the group that the prayer session has not failed if no words are spoken. Neither should there be pressure for everyone to speak if a few have begun to. That should enable people to relax more and therefore be more attentive to the Holy Spirit.

(iv) The person prayed for will know if other people's contributions and insights fit or not. If they don't appear to, then it may be that they are words to be stored up for another time (Luke 2.51). Remember that God is good and only wants the best for his children.

(v) Discourage anyone who wants to take over or dominate the group (see Chapter 13). It is important that each person who wants to speak has a fair innings.

(vi) Underline the importance of keeping confidences. There is something very destructive about laundering people's dirty washing in public. Concern for someone can so easily degenerate into gossip.

---

(2) Thy kingdom come, thy will be done

Introduction

In the phrase that is to be found in the Lord's Prayer, 'Thy kingdom come', there is a desire to become what God intended his creatures, his creation, to be.

When we pray 'Thy will be done', we are offering our will to be united with his, rather than spelling out a 'shopping list' of what *we* want him to do.

This exercise in intercession encourages us to share in God's intention that his creation should be fulfilled and everyone be healed and made whole.

131

Relaxation

Relax . . . let go of the tensions and anxieties which you may be carrying about . . . become aware of your breathing. . . . As always, we are in the presence of God, but now try to become aware of his presence. . . . He who made you and loves you is here with us now . . . around us . . . and within us . . . rest secure in his love for a while. . . .

Lifting others into God's presence

Now lift the person who is uppermost in your mind into this loving and healing presence . . . and hold them there, letting God's love shine on them. . . .

One by one, lift each of your loved ones into his presence in the same way. . . .

Now rest in God's love again, yourself. . . .

There may be people whom you find difficult, or who find you difficult – lift them now into God's presence and hold them there. No words are needed. . . .

Now rest in his love again. . . .

Lifting larger-scale concerns into God's presence

We have prayed for individuals, but we also have larger-scale concerns – lift to God the things happening in this country that worry you most – and ask that his will be done. . . .

Now move further afield and bring to God other parts of the world for which you have a special concern. . . .

And now, wider still, let us hold in God's presence our world with all its creatures, the planet we have been given to live on and to live in harmony with. . . .

You may find that you have used a lot of strength holding these large concerns to God, so come back and let his love envelop you again, let his strength fill you again. . . .

Lifting our neighbours into God's presence

Now, just wait quietly and be open, and see if the Holy Spirit brings someone else to your mind who needs your prayers. . . .

Finish by lifting the people on each side of you into God's loving and healing presence, and holding them there for a few minutes. . . .

ALL: Merciful Father,
accept these prayers
for the sake of your Son,
our Saviour Jesus Christ.
Amen.

(3) Interceding in the presence of God

To pray for people and the needs of the world is called intercession. For some people this is the only kind of prayer that they do but for others it is a form of prayer that seems particularly difficult. If God is almighty and all-knowing, what is the point of putting a person or situation before him? He knows what is going to happen anyway, so what is the point of asking? Also our personal knowledge and understanding of a particular person and/or situation may be so limited that we are not sure what to ask God for. We read in the Gospels how Jesus prayed for his disciples (Luke 22.31, John 17.19ff). He also taught them to pray. It is as if in some mysterious way God is inviting us to co-operate with him through prayer. Could it be that if we choose not to pray then we cause God's power in some measure to be withheld? God is calling us through his power to influence the course of events; to work with him to bring about his kingdom upon earth. Intercessory prayer is not a technique for changing God's mind, but it is a way of releasing God's power through our openness to his love and concern for his creation.

Many people see intercession as praying for the sick and suffering and an important part of intercession is just that. But it would be wrong to restrict our intercessions to those who suffer. This is a common fault of intercessory prayer groups and if you listen to the intercessions during Holy Communion in some churches you will notice that they suddenly come to life when they are praying for the sick. If our idea of God is that of a magic healer or wonder worker then it would seem natural to bring only the sick before him. But if we understand God as Creator of all that we know, who sees his creation as good and who is still working to bring his creation to completion, then we would naturally bring the whole of human life before the grace and direction of God.

Intercession is like all prayer, God-centred, but in intercession this fact needs to be stressed more strongly because so often we are in danger of focusing on the people we pray for instead of focusing on God and bringing the people, places and situations we wish to pray for into his presence.

(a) Make sure you are comfortable, so that your body feels cared for and does not need to clamour for attention in order to be comfortable.

(b) Concentrate on your breathing for a couple of minutes to become relaxed.

(c) Now become aware of God's presence, around you, between you and within you.

Imagine God's power and presence are flooding into you. Become aware of his very great love for you, the whole of you, just as you are. Keep your attention on God's presence, on your awareness of his love for you. (3 minutes)

(d) Now bring into his presence any situation or person you wish to pray for – just let them come one by one into your mind. In your imagination lift each situation or person into the presence of God. See them become filled with his power and love. Take as much time as you need. Don't hurry. Keep your attention focused on God as you lift those people and places who come into your mind into his presence.

Don't try to think deliberately of what to pray for, allow the Holy Spirit to suggest the people, nations, causes, situations to bring before God. If nothing comes, don't worry, just try to stay with an awareness of God's presence here with us and within you, breathing his light and life and power into you. (20 minutes)

End by saying a short prayer thanking God. This may take a few minutes if the silence has been deep.

(4) Robinsonian prayer – praying for individuals

The reason that it is called Robinsonian is that it is based on a method which can be found in John Robinson's book *Honest to God* (SCM Press 1963).

Introduction

You will need the following:
Any prayer list that you might use
Diary/engagement book
Address book
   or
The exercise can be done equally well with a newspaper or parish magazine.
Pencil and note-pad

Praying for individuals on your 'prayer list'

(a) You might begin by making a prayer of invocation of the Holy Spirit to help you to be sensitive to God's will.

(b) Examine the prayer list you have brought (if you don't use one, you might move straight on to your address book and draw one up; other names may be added).

Consider each of the names in turn. Do not hurry, and make sure that you have come to some kind of decision before you move on to the next. Consider what you can do for that person. Have you talked to them lately? Have you written to them lately? Do you know how they are? Do you even know where they are? In extreme cases do you even know who they are? (20 minutes)

– Consider what you can do for them.
– Consider how you can find out what you can do for them – make a note to ask them, if you feel this is appropriate.
– Consider if what you think you should do for them is likely to coincide with what they think you should do for them (and refrain from assuming that God would agree with you rather than with them!).
– Decide to do it.
– Enter it in your diary to be done on a given day at a given time. (If 'all' you can do is pray for them set aside some real time for that.) (15 minutes)

At the end of the session look at your prayer list again.

Formulate a series of rules which will result in:

– your never giving up praying for someone while there is something practical you can do for them;
– your considering anyone who remains on your list seriously every time you think of them;
– never having someone 'just on your prayer list';

– never letting anyone slip off your list inadvertently;
– committing to God's care those people for whom you can think of no appropriate action (as if they weren't there already) and putting them on a reserve list which you look at seriously in this same way once a quarter – or once a year – or whatever. (10 minutes)

Don't let it all get you down: think what God's filofax must look like.

○ (5) A specific agenda of intercession

Introduction

The method used here is loosely based on *The Inner Workings of a Prayer Cell* produced by the Lydia Prayer Fellowship. The heart of the session is intercession either taking up the concerns of the group or those that have been presented as the need before the meeting.

The advantage of this sort of exercise is that it has a structure (worship/Scripture; unburdening; intercession; thanksgiving) which some people find helpful, but there is also a freedom. The group may vary the length of each section as it feels appropriate.

Worship Ps. 138.1–2

Starting with a hymn, or choruses. This draws our attention and concentration 'heavenwards' as we remember that we are met in Jesus' name; it is a sacred time together, with Jesus as Lord in our midst. We recall it is his group, his time, and sometimes a passage of Scripture seems appropriate. We acknowledge we need the Holy Spirit to help us to pray.

Unburdening Ps. 66.18; 2 Cor. 10.5

Because of the frailty of our humanity, and because most prayer groups meet in the evening, it seems good to acknowledge to God our tiredness, our exhaustion with the day's affairs, our irritation, anger, fear, our negativity, and to receive his forgiveness as we forgive others, and receive all that he wants to give us of his peace, love, joy.

The leader might say a short prayer leaving a moment of silence for people privately to put down their burdens and problems. It is worth taking a few minutes to allow people to unload. (Some may want to do this aloud, but this should be discouraged here as it takes too long and it is important to allow everyone enough time to receive from God all that is needed in terms of forgiveness, refreshment of the Holy Spirit, so that the group might intercede together – see above, page 130, for unburdening).

Intercession Rom. 8.26; Acts 13.2

People may now feel free to pray as they are led by the Spirit, though the Spirit may lead the group into silence. It is usually helpful for everyone to focus on one subject at a time before moving on to the next. This may have been decided on beforehand, or else arise in the group – an openness and listening to God may lead in any direction. Occasionally the intercession may be seen in terms of a spiritual battle, and if so it may be good for the leader to enable those praying to feel surrounded by the overwhelming love of God by using appropriate prayers.

Thanksgiving and praise

Closing prayers and hymns or choruses again acknowledge that God is God – honour and glory, praise and worship belong to God and we can humbly offer no less. Finally the group could stand up, hold hands in a circle, and keeping their eyes open say the Grace, trying to have eye-to-eye contact with everyone else in the group. Then the peace might be exchanged.

(6) Healing. . . . is that what you really want?

Take time to be comfortable and relax then use John 5.1–18 for a meditation. Note that Jesus asks the question ('Do you want to get well?') and the patient has the responsibility of verbalizing desire and checking motivations. How many conflicting emotions and evasions are evident in the account as it is given in John? (Use the Good News Bible.)

Note other instances where Jesus makes the 'patient' look at what is being requested to clarify want, need, and desire, e.g. Matt. 20.20,21. The wife of Zebedee came – 'What do you want?' Jesus asked her. Matt. 20.32 (blind men). Jesus stopped and called them. 'What do you want me to do for you?' he asked them. Note also 'want' in Mark 5.6, 7 (the demoniac to Jesus): 'What do you want with me?' and in Matt. 15.28, Jesus to the woman – 'You are a woman of great faith. What you want will be done for you.'

Recapitulate this first section and appropriate what has been given.

HEALING . . . the promise

John 10.10 I have come in order that you might have life – life in all its fullness.

John 8.31 If you obey my teaching, you are really my disciples; and you will know the truth, and the truth will set you free.

Isa. 61 He has chosen me and sent me
To bring good news to the poor,
To heal the broken-hearted,
To announce release to captives
And freedom to those in prison.

Meditate on the relationship between healing and freedom in God's promise, and share insights.

HEALING . . . blocks to facing truth/freedom/wholeness.

Self-conscious striving

A brilliant young man desired the knowledge of all life. He went to the Grand Master and he pleaded to be taught. He asked, 'How long will it take me to learn it?' Now the Master had never been faced with such a question before and, in his momentary confusion, he said the first thing that came to his lips, 'Ten years!' The man was dismayed. With all his energy, enthusiasm and tremendous zeal, he asked again: 'Master, but what if I work twice as hard?' The Master looked at him and replied: 'Then it will take you twenty years!'

Focus on relief of pain

The experience of illness can serve as a stimulus for a growing sense of personal responsibility for one's own health. To focus on relief of pain alone may in the long run impair a patient's ability to acquire the skill needed to be a more responsible person.

Plato saw this integrative relationship twenty-five centuries ago when he wrote, 'The cure of many diseases is unknown to the physicians of Hellas because they are ignorant of the whole which ought to be studied also: for the part can never be whole unless the whole is well.'

Playing evasive games with God

Look again at John 5.1–18 and compare it with John 4.5–26. In the first the man sidesteps the question 'Do you want to get well?' by playing for time. The implications of being well may indeed outweigh the advantages of being sick. In the second the woman sidesteps the issue of her lifestyle which Jesus was questioning by changing the subject to prayer and religion. Even prayer can be used to evade facing the truth!

HEALING . . . conclusion.

Acts 4.11, 12. (Peter and John before the Council)

Jesus is the one of whom the Scripture says, 'The stone that the builders despised turned out to be the most important of all.' Salvation is to be found through him alone; in all the world there is no one else whom God has given who can save us.

Salvation = wholeness = freedom = truth.

John 14.6: 'I am the way, the truth, and the life.'

Finish with a Christ-centred prayer of thanksgiving.

Local intercession

The next two exercises are designed to address the issue of praying in the local situation, making us more aware of its needs – it's a routine maintenance sort of prayer instead of prayer based on local crisis. Only one could be done at any particular session. If the second one is chosen ask group members to bring their diaries to the session.

Resources

  Either
- large pieces of paper and felt-tip pens
- pens and paper
  or
- diary
- pens and paper

○ (7)   A local intercessory prayer cycle

The aim is to produce a prayer cycle. It may take several meetings to achieve. It may need a continuing process of updating.

Give each group member the task of listing on a piece of paper what they think are the appropriate headings for prayer in the church/parish/neighbourhood. (15 minutes)

Pool the headings. Together identify the gaps.

Can the group fill in some detail under each heading? What might be prayed for?

Who might be able to tell the group more about these areas of activity? Each group member commits him/herself to interview one of these people to obtain more information before the next meeting.

Spend some time praying your headings.

○ (8)   Intercession and the daily routine

Each group member is asked to write down on a piece of paper (from their diary if they use one) the church/community events/work situation in which they will be involved in the coming week/month. What are their hopes and anxieties about these events? (15 minutes)

Share the information in pairs. (10 minutes)

Then each pair holds hands and

quietly offers the hopes/anxieties of the partners to God. (5 minutes)

Share the experience of the wider group. Are there some events to which more than one group member is going? Are their hopes/anxieties similar or different? How can they support each other? How can the group support members facing anxieties/hopes on their own? (15 minutes)

(9)   When prayer is difficult

Introduction

Everyone has days when prayer seems difficult. There are times when we seem unable to concentrate, when distractions continually draw the mind away from our intention. The pressure of a particular worry, anxiety about

139

the future, the need for a difficult decision, can interfere with a genuine desire to pray. At such times, the deep need to come close to God for peace and help can in fact create tension which makes the attainment harder. And, if we are honest, we must admit that there are times when the desire is simply not there and we would rather be doing something else.

It is important not to allow guilt to drive us further into depression. We are coming in prayer to a loving Father, not to a tyrant who demands a period of homage or a troublesome old relative from whom we have future expectations. We need not get too pretentious about 'spiritual dryness' or 'the dark night of the soul': such longer alienation can be a reality of an intense spiritual life, but for most of us the bad times are temporary and have specific causes.

What is true for an individual may also be true for a group, which may have the same difficulties. There may be the burden of a big problem that all are carrying, or trouble which afflicts one or more of the members and involves the rest, or unresolved tensions within the group.

Whether the block is individual or collective, it is vital to stay committed to the period of prayer. The discipline of prayer is essential, not because God demands it arbitrarily but because we need it. The habit is strengthened by each observance and weakened by each refusal. Therefore we should use the time set aside, and not expect it always to be filled with exciting personal experiences.

Staying with the problem can be valuable and help us to hold on to the assurance that it will not go on for ever. Sometimes we need to know that God is not remote from our pain, but is alongside us in it and feels it too! We also need to give ourselves permission to opt out if we don't feel up to tackling it in the group setting. On the other hand the prayer might be used by an individual as well.

The words of Scripture can speak for us when our own prayer will not come.

The following is a possible framework for prayer which might help us to trust when things are not going well:

(a) Take whatever posture of prayer is most useful: the body can at least be at rest even if the mind is active.

(b) Remember that the very idea of prayer comes from God's calling. We should not be in this state of unfulfilled desire if he had not already brought us into his service. Our being present – the act of will involved – is in itself an act of faith, and a beginning in prayer. Rest for a time in that certainty, without being afraid of the distracting thoughts.

(c) If it helps, write down some of the things that trouble you: to verbalize and record them can make them less terrifying. Allow 5 minutes for this.

(d) Then slowly with pauses between each phrase say the texts below or similar ones appropriate to the situation. Each of the following sections might take about 7 minutes.

'They who wait for the Lord shall renew their strength' (Isa. 40.31 RSV).
'Be still and know that I am God' (Ps. 46.10 RSV).
'Come to me all who labour and are heavy laden, and I will give you rest' (Matt. 11.28 RSV).
'Fear not, little flock' (Luke 12.32 RSV).
'Peace I leave with you, my peace I give unto you: not as the world gives, do I give to you' (John 14.27 RSV).

(e) Try and open yourself to God, who is both the author and the goal of all prayer. Praise and adore him simply for all that he is: he is far greater than anything we can say to him or about him. Simply accept his presence in the way that is most real and comforting: the loving, powerful Father; Jesus the healing Son; the Holy Spirit who fills all things, who dwells within us and renews us. Now use words of adoration to come closer to him.

'For dominion belongs to the Lord, and he rules over the nations' (Ps. 22.28 RSV).

'O give thanks unto the Lord; for he is good: because his mercy endureth for ever' (Ps. 118.1 AV).
'Christ in you, the hope of glory' (Col. 1.27 AV).
'Looking unto Jesus, the author and finisher of our faith' (Heb. 12.2 AV).
'The spirit of glory and of God resteth upon you' (1 Pet. 4.14 AV).

(f) In this assurance, let all anxieties come into the open. Make the distractions from prayer into the prayer-offering for the day. Our weakness and insufficiency are as good as prayer, because they are honest. There is nothing real to us that we cannot hold up in prayer to God. It is not necessary to make all our petitions in solemn forms or to be sure that we are asking for the right things.

Now imagine yourself standing at the foot of the cross and laying down burdens which God will take up and transform into what is best for you.

'Out of the depths have I cried unto thee, O Lord' (Ps. 130.1 AV).
'Hear the voice of my supplications when I cry unto thee' (Ps. 28.2 AV).
'In everything by prayer and supplication with thanksgiving let your requests be made known unto God' (Phil. 4.6 AV).
'The Spirit itself maketh intercession for us' (Rom. 8.26 AV).
'Your Father knoweth what things ye have need of before ye ask him' (Matt. 6.8 AV).

(g) Rest in the love that is always there. Feel it as a bright light which illumines all things, a warm radiance spread through all creation. Whatever we have known of joy and happiness is a little experience of what God has prepared for us. And even in this world, joy will be ours again on another day.

'The eternal God is thy refuge, and underneath are the everlasting arms' (Deut. 33.27 AV).

'Eye hath not seen, nor ear heard, neither have entered into the heart of man, the things which God hath prepared for them that love him' (1 Cor. 2.9 AV).

'Let not your heart be troubled' (John 14.1 or 27 AV).

'I am come that they might have life, and that they might have it more abundantly' (John 10.10 AV).

'God is love' (1 John 4.8 AV).

Hold to this love for the appointed time and then say:

> Go in peace
> to love and serve the Lord.

You have 'said your prayers': the bad day has been a step forward in faith.

(10) Prayer for global issues

Introduction

This exercise gives a form of prayer for the needs of the world. Often people get overwhelmed by the scale of the problems and can't grapple with prayer about big world issues so they abandon it. The prayer is set out in three parts, each lasting perhaps 15 minutes.

Praise

(a) Imagine that you have put a great distance between yourself and planet earth. You are out in space and viewing the earth from a long way off. Watch it slowly turning on its axis. Observe:

> the land masses;
> the polar ice caps;
> the oceans;
> each continent in turn.

Take as long as you need to do this. Now look at it again with love and listen to the words: 'God saw all that he had made, and it was very good' (Gen. 1.31 REB).

(b) Now imagine that you have come a little closer. You can see more detail:

> desert regions of Africa, Central Asia, Australia;
> forests of N. Europe, Amazon and Central Africa;
> river plains of Punjab and Zambezi;
> mountainous regions like the Himalayas, Alps and Rockies.

Now look at them again with love and listen to the words: 'Lord, you have made so many things! How wisely you made them all! The earth is filled with your creatures' (Ps. 104.24 GNB).

(c) Now imagine you have come close enough to see even more:

some of the creatures on earth;
the oceans teeming with fish;
all kinds of living plants and trees;
you can also see men and women
made in God's likeness.

Look at it all again with love and
listen to the words: 'Yes, you love
everything that exists, you hold
nothing of what you have made in
abhorrence, for had you hated anything you would not have formed it'
(Anon).

Contrition

Now that you are nearer to the earth
you can begin to use your other
senses:

listen to the cries of the poor;
listen to the sounds of bombing;
smell the burning of forests;
smell the effluence and pollution
from toxic wastes.

You may choose a specific situation to
locate the prayer, e.g. a refugee camp,
a house in Soweto or on the West
Bank, a prison in Central America.
Look and listen to the plight of the
poor with sorrow and repentance and
say the following words: 'Be merciful
to me, O God, because of your constant love. Because of your great
mercy, wipe away my sins' (Ps. 51.1–2
GNB).

Intercession

Now return to the place where you
are praying. Imagine that Jesus is
present with you in the room where
you are praying. Ask for your needs
to be met, both as an individual and
as a member of a community.

Finish by saying the Grace.

*Blessed are those who love you, O God, and love their friends in you and their enemies for your
sake. They alone will never lose those who are dear to them, for they love them in One who is
never lost.*

ST AUGUSTINE

13
Leading a Prayer Group

People find themselves leading a prayer group for all sorts of reasons. Maybe they want to start one up. Maybe somebody wants them to start one up. Maybe they're a member of an existing group and suddenly the mantle of leadership falls upon them. Some can't wait to assume leadership, others can't wait to pass it on to somebody else! Some seem to have a natural gift for it, for others it's very hard work. Not everybody is designed by God to be a prayer group leader, and there's no disgrace in admitting that and declining to take on the role. But for those who, for whatever reason, find themselves in a leadership role, here are some hints of things to think about. Some of the points overlap with each other, and many of them will seem pretty obvious.

---

(1)   Who's the leader anyway?

It's not necessary for the same person always to lead the group. There's much value in leadership rotating within the group. Perhaps different people could lead different parts of the meeting?

However leadership is exercised there's a lot to be said for allowing the whole group to assess how the meetings are going, and to plan for the future. Not every time you meet, but from time to time. It means that responsibility for the group will be seen to rest with everybody, not just with one or two – for whom it can easily become a burden. It also means that it is less likely that any individual's needs will be forgotten.

If one person remains recognizably the leader, and there may be such a person even if the leadership of meetings is shared, then who supports them? Who do they talk to about how things are going?

Beware of members who seek to hijack the group: to dominate it or to impose their own personal agenda upon it.

---

(2)   When, where, and how often, to meet?

Is the group to meet for a specified number of occasions? Or is the implication that it will meet for ever? Perhaps agreeing to meet for a limited number of times, and then reviewing things together, is the best way.

Can anybody join? That may seem like a good idea; but the danger is that you'll get a group of people whose needs are very different, and perhaps incompatible. The alternative is to invite people to join; the danger of that is that you may seem elitist and exclusive to those not invited!

Is there an optimum size for the group? Eight to ten people seems a good number. But remember that not everybody will be present every time.

How long will the meetings last? It's a good idea to establish agreement about this, and then to end sharply at the appointed time. Some members may have other commitments.

Where to meet? A public place, like a church room, may be easier for people to come to, but may well be less comfortable than somebody's front room. Should you always meet in the same place, or should you move around to different venues? There are advantages and disadvantages either way.

---

(3) Getting things ready

The organization of the meeting itself merits careful thought.

The group needs to be clear what its task is. Are you meeting together to pray for world peace or to pray for those who are sick? Or are you wanting to explore different ways of praying? The group's task may change over a period of time. Again periodic opportunities for the group to review what its task is, is often helpful. It may be easiest to alert people at one meeting that there will be a review-time at the next, so that they have time to collect their thoughts. Some people are good at talking off the top of their head, others prefer time to think first!

It is probably very important to establish at the very beginning of the group meeting together, that anything that is said is to be treated as confidential.

Do you want to begin or end the meeting with tea or coffee? If so, make sure that refreshments are kept simple, so that providing them doesn't become a burden, and people do not feel they have to match the sumptuous spread provided at the last meeting! If you always meet in one member's home it may be appropriate to share the cost of refreshments.

How will you handle interruptions, such as the phone ringing, or the doorbell going, during the meeting? Can the phone be taken off the hook? Can someone be delegated to deal with any interruptions? There's nothing more disruptive than a series of outside interruptions.

How will the seating be arranged? A circle is often best unless the particular prayer exercise requires a different arrangement. Serried ranks before the leader's throne is not to be recommended. Some members may prefer a hard or a soft chair. Some may not want to sit at all! Soft, comfortable, unobtrusive lighting is much more relaxing than harsh lighting. It is astonishing how the 'feel' of the room in which you meet will make a difference.

It is often helpful to use music in a prayer group. If you do, it's very important to rehearse the logistics. Having to wait while the leader keeps fast forwarding the tape-recorder to try and find the piece of music required can be very irritating if you've just got yourselves quiet and settled. If you have more than one piece of music, can you put them on the same tape, one after the other, for ease of reproduction?

If you're using a Bible it may be helpful to agree beforehand which version you're going to use - even to the point of reproducing the text on a piece of paper for everybody. It may be fascinating to see how different versions vary but it may sidetrack people from the matter in hand.

---

(4) Here we go

It's usually a good idea at the very beginning of the meeting to explain simply what is going to happen, what will be expected of people, what they should be doing. If people know what is going to happen, for example, 'we will spend ten minutes doing this, and then fifteen minutes doing that', they feel more comfortable and able to participate, less self-conscious and anxious.

Make sure you never ask people to do things they can't do. If you have several things to do, always start with the easiest, to give people confidence. On the other hand don't be frightened, when it seems appropriate, to challenge people to try something new.

There is some merit in staying with the same pattern for most meetings, not to the point of total rigidity, but just so that people feel relaxed because they're familiar with the routine.

It's important to start the meeting by introducing people to each other - or better still get people to introduce themselves. It may also be helpful to provide a time when people can off-load the agenda that they've brought with them. If they're very worried about something they may need to share it before they can get down to prayer. Occasionally it may be appropriate to allow this to take over the whole meeting, and to use it as the basis of the group's prayer together.

More prosaically, if someone has had to rush home from work and grab something to eat before coming to the meeting, they'll need a few minutes just to unwind from all that. You can do that over coffee, or by having a few minutes quiet at the beginning of the meeting.

It may help to begin with a time of 'centring down' before moving on to the main agenda (see chapter 1). This time of relaxation, of being still before God, is a necessary prelude to prayer for some people.

You need to be sensitive to times of silence - giving people enough time, but not so much as to become oppressive. The simplest way may be to ask people how long they'd like silences to be.

It's nearly always helpful to end a prayer exercise with an opportunity for people to talk about what they've experienced – be it good or bad. Obviously nobody should be pressed to share anything they don't want to. Often it helps to split the group into twos to swop reflections before calling everybody back to bring anything appropriate to the wider group.

(5) We're not all the same

Never forget that every person in the group is different. The differences may arise out of a difference in churchmanship or denomination, or simply different personalities. A word that means one thing to one person may mean something else to another. Some will love the use of incense in prayer, whilst others won't. Some will want to pray out loud, others will prefer to be silent. Some are good with words, others are not. Some have lots of imagination, others have very little.

No one exercise is likely to be helpful to everybody present. That's a good reason for allowing the leadership of the group to rotate – everybody will have the opportunity of offering what they find helpful, and of having the validity of that offering confirmed by other people (a bit like this book!).

One of the prayer exercises that we received had been written by an Anglican clergyman for his church magazine at Christmastime. It offers eight different paths to the celebration of Jesus' birth. We reproduce it here. When you've read it through ask yourself which way appeals most to you, and which least? Can you think of people you know who would find helpful the ways that you didn't?

Many paths to Bethlehem: you can't go down them all

Here are eight ways of approaching the birth of the baby in Bethlehem. Please use what appeals to you and ignore what doesn't. We are all very different, because that's how God made us.

Using the imagination with the senses

Imagine that you are in Bethlehem, entering the stable. What will the sounds and the sights and the smells be? In your mind's eye go into the stable. What will you see? What will you touch and hear? Who else might be there? Just appreciate the presence of Mary and Joseph and Jesus and concentrate all the time on what you might see and hear, touch and smell and maybe even taste.

Using the freewheeling imagination

Imagine that you are there in Bethlehem. Just be present there and look at it all in your mind's eye. Then sit back and see what happens. Don't force your imagination along particular lines. Just let it freewheel and see what comes.

If you enjoyed the first approach, you may find the second uncongenial, and vice versa. Don't worry about it. Follow the way that is most natural for you.

Bringing Jesus into the present

Look back over today. Concentrate on one moment when you felt something strongly – pleasure, anger, affection, fear, any feeling which made quite an impression on you today. Go back in your mind's eye and just be there again, and let yourself experience the same emotion again. Maybe there was some reason why you felt like that. Take notice if there was. Don't worry if there wasn't. Then imagine that Bethlehem comes to you. The holy family are in the same place with you. Maybe Mary even hands you the baby to hold. What will you feel then? If you could make one request to him, what would you say, feeling all that you have felt today? If that baby could speak to you, what would he ask you to be, or think, or do?

Praying with your pen or paintbrush

You are the editor of the *Bethlehem Star*. What articles will there be in your paper? What will be the headlines and what the small articles? Would the birth, the shepherds, the wise men be the major articles in the real world of that day? How would you as editor arrange what is in your paper?

Don't worry if you're not good enough to exhibit your work. Borrow your children's crayons or paints and doodle around the idea of the birth of Jesus.

Praying from words

Take the story in Luke or Matthew or the philosophical introduction to John and just read them slowly. If you can do it without family or friends thinking you've gone mad, read the words aloud quietly. When a particular word or phrase hits you, stop and chew on it in your heart. Maybe say some words of prayer to God as well. When this stops being useful for you, just read on a little further until something hits you again.

Retell the story of Jesus for today

Imagine Jesus born in our world. Where today would you find a people or a group who were oppressed in a similar way to Jesus' family and nation? What would be the equivalent

151

of the census? Of Herod? Of the stable? Who would in our day take the place of the outcast shepherds and the powerful wise men? And who are the angels (and 'angels' means 'messengers') bringing 'tidings of great joy which shall be to all people'?

Light a candle and look at it

Just sing

Let yourself get lost singing the Christmas hymns and songs, out loud or in your head, and be aware of Jesus.

And when we have done any of these devotional exercises, let us remember the many ways that Jesus meets us – in the mystery of the bread and wine, in the words of the gospel, in the fellowship of all believers, and in the cry of the needy. And wherever we encounter our incarnate Lord.

O COME LET US ADORE HIM.

14
Praying through Lent: Advice for Prayer Group Leaders

One of the strengths of this book, we hope, is its variety and flexibility. But for some people that very variety may be a cause of bafflement and confusion. The aim of this final chapter is to help those who find it difficult to know how to get started.

We suggest that you *begin* by reading chapter 13, 'Leading a Prayer Group'.

Next, talk about how you're going to proceed with someone who has had some experience in leading prayer groups.

You will need to give careful thought to how your group is set up. If it's an already existing group, then the members will need to agree to have prayer as their focus for the duration of the course. Would they be willing for new members to join for this period? And if so, how would those new members do so? Most important, is there a natural starting point for the group, for example, prayer and the Bible, intercession healing, contemplative prayer . . .? In which case, the group could start with an exercise from the appropriate chapter of this book. Or does the group want simply to explore new ways of praying? If so, how are the new ways chosen? By the leader? Collectively? Another question to be tackled is, should the group have a permanent leader, or will the leadership of the group change with each meeting, with each new leader taking responsibility for his/her own session, and the book being passed round?

Most of these questions will also need to be thought about if the group is a new group. It is most important clearly to establish what the *aim* of the group is. Unless you are clear about this you are most unlikely to achieve your aim, not least because you'll attract members whose aims are very different. It is astonishing how many groups (and not just prayer groups) come to grief primarily because these basic organizational questions have not been thought through and resolved. Hence our emphasis on the value of the leader having somebody outside the group with whom he or she can discuss these questions.

Some possible outlines for a Five-Week Lent course

Note: The figures in brackets following an exercise refer to the chapter number and the exercise number.

1. You may have a declared starting point – in which case you will want to start in the appropriate chapter, and perhaps even to stay there, through the course.

2. This outline starts with prayer and the Bible, and develops a Lenten theme:
SESSION 1 'Praying the Scriptures' (3/1) – you may like to use the Gospel for the 1st Sunday in Lent
SESSION 2 'The Transfiguration' (3/6)
SESSION 3 One of the liturgical exercises offering Reconciliation (7/1–5)
SESSION 4 Either 'Prayer for Global Issues' (12/10), or 'Movement in Prayer', perhaps using the walk as being with Jesus on the way to Jerusalem (11/3)
SESSION 5 'Contrasting Images' (9/2)

3. This outline seeks to explore new ways of praying:
SESSION 1 One of the 'centring down' exercises, e.g. 'Leads into Silence' (1/1–4). If more material is needed almost anything could be used, e.g. 'Listening' (11/6)
SESSION 2 One of the intercessory exercises, e.g. 'Robinsonian Prayer' (12/4) or 'Thy Kingdom Come' (12/2)
SESSION 3 A journalling exercise, e.g. 'Twenty-Four Hours' (8/4)
SESSION 4 An exercise from chapter 2, 'Prayer in the Midst of Life', e.g the 'Slot' Prayer (2/5), or a more imaginative exercise, e.g 'Meditation on a Stone' (10/3) or 'Choose your own object' (10/4)

SESSION 5 Either a reconciliation exercise, e.g. 'Forgiven and Free' (7/1), or something from the Adoration section, e.g. 'An exercise in coming to God as we are' (5/2) or 'Except you become as little children' (4/4)

These course outlines are only suggestions. Feel free to change them, to modify them, or to ignore them altogether.

Appendix

SPIDIR

was founded in 1979 and is an informal and ecumenical network of people practising or interested in the work of spiritual direction.

To this end it

(1) lays on day conferences and workshops on topics related to spiritual direction;
(2) publishes a newsletter three times a year;
(3) has a programme of learning for spiritual directors;
(4) provides a contact and information focus for the work of spiritual direction.

Membership

(1) The subscription year runs from January to December. Reminders are sent with the Autumn Newsletter.
(2) Full membership costs £5.00 and includes mailings and half-price entry to SPIDIR conferences.
(3) Associate membership costs £2.00 (mailings only).

All enquiries regarding SPIDIR membership should be made to Mrs Paddy Lane, 51 Lime Tree Grove, Shirley, Croydon CR0 8AZ.

Comments and contributions to the Newsletter are

welcome. Please send them to the editor: The Revd Tony Lucas, St George's Rectory, Manciple Street, London SE1 4LW.
Chair: Mrs Janet Unwin, 9 Dover Park Drive, London SW15 5BT.

Henry Morgan, former chairman of SPIDIR, is an Anglican priest who now exercises a freelance ministry, which enables him to be available to others who want to grow in their own spiritual lives. He works with The Annunciation Trust and can be contacted at 4 Glebe Gardens, New Malden, Surrey KT3 5RY.